Owner's Guide To
Better
Behavior
In Dogs

Owner's Guide To
Better
Behavior
In Dogs
Second Edition

William E. Campbell
Ilustrated by Robert M. Miller

Alpine
Blue Ribbon Books

Alpine Publications, Inc., Loveland, Colorado

Owner's Guide to Better Behavior in Dogs

ISBN 0-931866-64-2

Library of Congress Cataloging-in-Publication Data

Campbell, William E. (William Edward). 1929-
    Owner's guide to better behavior in dogs / by William E. Campbell
    illustrated by Robert M. Miller.
    280 p.   cm.
    Includes bibliographical references and index.
    ISBN 0-931866-64-2
    1. Dogs—Behavior.   2. Dogs—Training.   I. Title   II. Title:
    Better behavior in dogs.
    SF4433.C3525   1994
    636. 7'0887- - dc20   93-36753
                                                                  CIP

Cover Photo by Faith Uridel. Ch. Winterwheat's Illusive Glance,
    ("Jamie") number one Soft Coated Wheaten bitch in 1991 and 1992.
Cover Design: Bob Schram
Layout: B. J. McKinney

  2 3 4 5 6 7 8 9 0

Printed in the United States of America.

TABLE OF CONTENTS

vi

PART IV   WHEN YOU NEED MORE HELP

Acknowledgments

Thanks to tens of thousands of my dedicated clients, their fascinating pets, and the thousands of forward-looking veterinarians whose referrals have been bringing us together since 1967.

John P. Scott and the late John L. Fuller for their tireless work and selfless sharing of ideas in their landmark book, Dog Behavior, The Genetic Basis.

Michael Fox, veterinarian/behaviorist, who sparked behavior interest among so many veterinarians in the 1960s.

Dare Miller, who introduced me to this field and pioneered an etiological approach to behavior problems in dogs.

Fred Smithcors, DVM, Ph.D., for selecting me as contributing editor to Modern Veterinary Practice magazine in 1972 and who published the first edition of Behavior Problems in Dogs.

Paul Pratt, DVM, publisher, American Veterinary Publications, who made the second edition possible.

Betty Jo McKinney, publisher, Alpine Publications, for seeing the value of revising this book.

Special thanks to "Tally," our Dalmatian and "Randy," our Norwegian Elkhound, who unselfishly shared their lives with us as part of our family and indispensable members of our behavioral team.

Thanks: To RMA. You have brought to our visual senses, with humor, the essence of our ideas.

And to my patient, understanding wife, Peggy. She is more important than I can say.

About the Author

Bill Campbell's early background was in TV and radio writing and broadcasting. Later, after training in industrial psychology, he conducted human motivation programs for seven years.

Bill worked for four years with Dave Miller, Ph.D., at the Canine Behavior Institute in Los Angeles. He later established the Dog Owner Guidance Service at Sun Valley Ranch. He became a contributing editor of *Modern Veterinary Practice* magazine, and in 1975 published *Behavior Problems in Dogs*. That year he helped found the American Society of Veterinary Ethology.

Bill and his wife, Peggy, now live on a wooded ranch near Grants Pass, Oregon. Bill lectures, consults and writes for *Modern Veterinary Practice*, *Dog World*, and other publications. He and Peggy market the *BehavioRx* series of dog and cat behavior brochures, which are available from many veterinary hospitals.

About the Illustrator

Dr. Bob Miller (RMM) cartooned his way through the Colorado State University School of Veterinary Medicine, graduating in 1956. He has practiced in Thousand Oaks, California, ever since, where his daily practice experiences serve as inspiration for his cartoons and writing. American Veterinary Publications (Santa Barbara, CA) has published five books of his cartoons and comic verse. His cartoons have appeared regularly in *Modern Veterinary Practice* and other magazines, and he writes a monthly column for *Veterinary Medicine*. In 1985 his autobiographical book, *Most of My Patients are Animals* (Paul S. Ericksson, Middlebury, VT) was published, with an introduction by his friend and colleague, James Herriot.

Foreword

When Bill Campbell's *Owner's Guide to Better Behavior in Dogs &
Cats* first came out in 1989, I had the pleasure of reviewing it for
"Pure Bred Dogs--The American Kennel Gazette," the official publica-
tion of the American Kennel Club. I liked it then and I like the revised
edition even better. It is a pleasure to read, and the delightful cartoon-
style drawings by R. M. Miller, DVM immeasurably enhance its appeal. It is a great book to help owners understand their charges. Every
pet owner will benefit from this book; anyone who advises pet owners
needs to study it. Both need to keep it handy as a permanent reference
source.

Unlike the vast majority of books dealing with either behavior
problems in dogs or dog training, this one advocates an approach to
unwanted or objectionable behavior that does not automatically assume it is the dog's fault. It looks at behavior and so-called behavior
problems from the pet's perspective and seeks to get the owner actively involved in a mutually beneficial resolution.

Dogs are such popular pets because they have so many seemly human qualities. It is for this reason owners tend to anthropomorphize--
they attribute human properties to pets which they do not possess,
such as guilt, shame, sense of duty, or knowing right from wrong. Inevitably, this leads to major misunderstandings and handling the pet
in the wrong way. Bill Campbell explains dogs indeed do think. Often,
what the dog does is not only perfectly normal from the dog's point of
view, but necessary for its mental health. Once the owner understands the reason for the pet's action, a humane plan of corrective action can be employed.

Clearly explained are the influences early experiences have on
shaping the adult pet's behavior. Also explained are how the dog's environment and the owner's interaction can cause behavior problems
and how to solve these. One of my own personal pet peeves is ad-

dressed as well: contrary to popular belief, dogs do not lie awake at night thinking of ways to get back at their owners. Instead, owners, quite unintentionally, but equally systematically train their dogs to behave the way they do. Once the owner is made aware of how he or she affects the dog's actions, logical solutions follow.

Whatever behaviors you find objectionable on the part of your pet, you will find the explanation in this book. You will also learn how to deal with these behaviors without violating your pet's dignity and sense of self worth. If you apply the principles contained in this book, your pet will reward you by being the perfect companion you always wanted.

Jack Volhard
Author of numerous articles,
senior author of four books, and
co-producer of four video tapes
on dog training.
Phoenix, New York

Introduction

The symbiotic relationship between man and dog goes back to the earliest phases of mankind's development. Both creatures were hunters. Both lived in small groups—a band or pack—and both were governed by a complex social order. Both species lived by their wits, lacking the physical power of the great predators such as the lion and sabre-toothed tiger, and used strategy and the strength of numbers to bring home game. The puppy fit into the primitive cave domicile, serving as a playmate for human children, an entertaining companion for the adults, and was the source and recipient of affection and stroking. The dog's keener senses were invaluable to man in guarding his territory, and in locating, pursuing and bringing down game. Much later, when man became a pastoral nomad, the dog herded his flocks. The fact that man often abused the dog, and sometimes ate him, doesn't alter the intensely close relationship between the two species. Thus, man and dog have an extremely long and traditional relationship. Most people instinctively like dogs. Watch a toddler as a friendly dog approaches. Observe people of all ages as they crowd up to the pet shop window. The dog is historically secure in this place as man's best friend.

The sciences of human psychology and human behavior are a mere century old. The sciences of animal behavior and ethology (comparative behavior) are much younger. We are only beginning to understand that each species inherits behavioral characteristics peculiar to it, which helped that species to survive and develop in a hostile environment. There are many differences between the inherent behavioral characteristics of man and dog. Our imprinting and learning patterns differ. We signal aggression, submission, territorial possession, the desire to play, and the desire to mate in very different ways. Yet, as we shall see in Bill Campbell's excellent and perceptive book, there are many similarities between our behavior and that of our canine friends.

Campbell's techniques go beyond the usual dog training rote and often fallacious methods. He examines, understands and uses the dog's inherent responses to produce a well-adjusted dog. One of life's greatest pleasure, indeed, is a mannerly and well-adjusted dog. Most of us know that and crave such a relationship. Too often, however, things don't go as we had hoped, and it can be a great problem, a stress, a liability, and even a danger. This book brings to the average literate dog owner an understanding of basic canine behavior, together with techniques to produce a well-mannered and happy dog.

R. M. Miller, DVM
Thousand Oaks, California

Preface

This book presents the lessons I've learned during the past twenty-seven years. It describes how dogs think, how they develop socially, and why they behave as they do. Then it looks at how people, usually unwittingly, create problems for pets and themselves. A typical problem case history follows, which shows how the behavioral principles are applied. Finally, it presents specific, humane correction programs that have been dispensed by thousands of veterinarians for more than a decade and that have been used successfully by hundreds of thousands of dog owners.

People don't want to inflict pain or emotional stress on their dogs. All they really want is for the dog to come when called, to sit and stay when told, and to otherwise stay out of trouble; for instance, to not chew up shoes, poop or pee in the house, jump on guests, bite the mailman, or run into the street and get killed.

If you have raised a dog before, you know that good behavior from a puppy or older dog doesn't happen automatically. Dogs are a lot like babies and children. They chew in order to teethe or taste things. They have to be taught where (and when) to go to the bathroom. They love to run around wildly and jump to develop their motor skills. When they reach the canine teens (about four to six months), they often start barking to warn of visitors or noises from outside their territory. This stage of maturation marks the beginning of their drive to do a job; to work as a member of the group.

During all phases of life, the way in which a dog is treated influences his future behavior and, hence, the quality of relationships with them. In the first six months of life, most pups reach sexual maturity, while a human baby usually requires more than ten years. With such rapid maturation, it is especially important to avoid treatment that may produce psychological trauma or other stressful experiences that can erupt as serious behavioral problems later in life.

Our family dogs don't choose us. We choose them. And, if they misbehave, they need only three things from us - Our understanding of why, nonabusive corrections that reflect our insight about the nobler instinctive and learned behaviors of humans and dogs. That is what this book is all about.

William E. Campbell
Grants Pass, Oregon

UNDERSTANDING YOUR DOG

Reader Aids

These symbols tell you where to find especially helpful information. Look for:

 NOTE OF INTEREST
Information on dog behavior and/or how to better understand your dog.

 TIP:
Pointers and training tips to which you may want to refer again and again.

How Your Dog Thinks

Whether you are trying to house-train a new puppy, correct an adult dog from wetting in the house, or solve a destructive chewing problem, you will succeed more quickly if you understand how your dog thinks, because you will appreciate how he learns. With this knowledge, you can recognize and avoid abusive treatment and apply humane corrections that communicate naturally and effectively.

Communication Between Dogs and People

It is important that you analyze and clarify the exact nature of the communication interchange between you and your pet. Precious little goes on between you and your dog that can be termed "intellectual" in a human sense. That is, you cannot discuss with your dog the upcoming day's activities or how you feel about the state of the economy. The closest thing to intelligent interchange is your dog's uncanny ability to manipulate you by the way in which he behaves toward you. Your demand on the pet's intelligence may be asking him to learn a few simple commands and to teach concepts like "right" and "wrong." In short, most dogs use their intelligence with relative efficiency. Most owners do not. When you take a statistical look at who emerges as the superior teacher, the dog wins hands down.

The major content, or quality, of the relationship between you and your pet is *emotional*. You enjoy your dog when he makes you *feel good*. You don't enjoy him when his behavior makes you *feel bad*. It is the same from the dog's point of view. However, a dog applies his intelligence to satisfy his emotions more diligently than you do. If you apply the principles presented here, **you** can become the superior teacher and, therefore, provide competent leadership for the dog.

Ideas About Dogs and Thinking

An ancient Chinese sage said, "There is much of man in the animal, and all of the animal in man." In this proverb, "man" signifies mankind, not just male humans! Dog owners, and some animal behaviorists, are often criticized by behavioral scientists for projecting human qualities onto animals. In spite of this, humans and dogs do share an exceptional number of similarities in their emotional make-up. While we may try to separate emotion from pure intelligence, each affects the other in important ways.

Let's look at some ideas about dogs and thinking. We first have to ask if dogs think at all. Some experts claim that dogs don't think, they merely behave. The popular definitions of thinking, "*to form or have in mind*" or "*intend, plan*" certainly fit the way dogs behave. Dogs *plan* to get some petting when they approach and nudge us for it. They *have in mind* greeting us when they wag their tails and go to the door upon hearing our car pull into the garage. They may not think in the complex, abstract ways humans do, but they certainly think.

James McConnell, the teacher-scientist who studied flatworms, contended, "If you're going to study flatworm behavior, you'd better learn to think like a flatworm." He evidently mastered the art, too, because he made landmark contributions to understanding intelligence and the mechanics of learning in *all* animals.

One thing seems certain, dogs don't think in verbal language. They never sit around in groups making well-defined noises as if having a chat. The noises they make are usually emotional expressions or attempts to gain attention, as in barking angrily at another dog approaching their property, or woofing at the back door to get us to let them into the house. So, if they don't think in words, what do they use?

Images and the Senses

The most appealing evidence suggests that *dogs think in visual images and other sensory impressions, such as sounds and odors.* This is not to say that they sit around experiencing videos inside their brains. However, they very likely share our ability to form images in their minds and experience certain odors and sounds.

The scientific observations behind this idea, published in the United States in 1973, come from a Russian scientist named V. S. Rusinov, who was studying the electrophysiology of the brain. Several

of his dogs were permanently wired with brain-wave equipment and radio transmitters that conveyed data to electroencephalograph (EEG) machines. When the dogs were brought into the lab for experimental learning tests, the EEG machine was turned on to record their brain-wave patterns. This was done at the same time each day, five days a week.

One weekend, purely by accident, Rusinov brought a group of visitors into the lab and turned on the EEG machine. The dogs scheduled for tests on weekdays were sending wave forms from their outside kennel that were nearly identical to Rusinov's weekday laboratory working patterns! When the regular testing time passed, the dogs' brain waves returned to their normal "at rest" forms. I never found any mention by Rusinov whether the dogs out in the kennel were actually *performing* their laboratory conditioned behaviorisms. Chances are they were not, but one thing is almost certain–they were apparently experiencing them mentally. Rusinov's work also showed that his dogs kept a biological clock that was accurate to within thirty seconds in a twenty-four-hour period!

In other work, the late Polish scientist, Jerzi Konorski, taught dogs to salivate and expect food in their trays when a light flickered. This was tested every few minutes. However, after a few trials, the dogs started salivating and looking at the trays as if the food was there, though the light had not flickered. Konorski ventured that the dogs thought they were seeing (hallucinating) both the stimuli (the light) and the reward for salivating (the food). One thing is sure–something was happening in the dogs' minds that made them *behave* as if it were happening.

Human Imagery Examples

To better appreciate the dog's situation, think about our own mind's eye. Imagine we are to meet someone we are particularly fond of at a busy restaurant. We arrive a few minutes early and sit at a table near the door. The appointed time goes by and we begin to wonder if he or she might have forgotten the date. We start getting worried. We start watching as people approach the door. Soon, strangers who merely have similar builds, hair color, or facial features almost cause us to call out our friend's name. This phenomenon occurs because the strangers with similarities to our friend's features nearly fit our own mental image of the friend. Most of us have had such experiences.

Sometimes just thinking about a loved one conjures up a mental image of that person. This applies to the sound of his or her voice as well. Think about your favorite musical piece and you can almost "hear" it. These are *examples of positive images* that are *emotionally pleasant*. On the other hand, recalling a terrifying experience cannot only recreate its image, but also make us shudder. This exemplifies a *negative image* that is *emotionally unpleasant*.

It is probably the same for our dogs. When we are late getting home, especially if they miss us too much because we have spoiled them, it is likely they worry in images. They recall images of us fluffing the pillows on the sofa, putting away record albums, handling magazines and books, putting on shoes just before leaving, or sitting in a favorite armchair. As a result, when we are gone, they often engage in activities that involve them with these articles or activities: pillows pulled onto the floor, albums or magazines moved or chewed, a chair seat dug up, shoes brought out of the closet and taken to the door through which the owner usually returns home. *The dogs want the owners' presence and try to experience things that symbolize them.*

To see how this fits in life, consider the new puppy whose owner comes home from work and joins in the ecstatic joy of the typical greeting ceremony. As this becomes ingrained, the pup begins anticipating the experience. As will happen, one day the owner is late. The pup's biological clock says they should be home, so he begins fretting and pacing. Well-primed energies begin demanding an outlet. What's going on in his mind? Probably, he imagines hearing footsteps, per-

The dog gets uptight and tense when the house is like a morgue.

haps even seeing the door open, which doesn't happen this time. This introduces a conflict between what the dog expects and the reality he is experiencing. Conflict creates frustration. Frustration produces anxiety, which in turn produces a rush of activity-producing adrenaline. The pup searches for something to satisfy his desire to "experience" the owner. He comes upon a book rich with the owner's scent that he saw the owner reading recently. If the pup cannot have the owner personally, he can at least have his or her odor or taste. So he sniffs, tastes, sometimes even swallows parts of the article. Unfortunately, this provides only temporary relief.

Then the owner comes home. The puppy launches into his joyous, semi-hysterical ritual. The owner starts to join in, but spies the shredded book. What's this! Quite naturally, if not wisely, the owner angrily grabs the pup, drags him to the pulverized object and scolds him, or slaps his muzzle or rump, or both. The pet's single-track mind is riveted on the owner as he yips, rolls over, or tries vainly to escape. The owner, growling, picks up the remnants of the book and storms to the trash basket. The confused pup now has a brand new *conflicting image of its owner.*

This kind of shock to the nervous system, in animals and humans, is called *psychic trauma.* A conflict occurs between the usually *positive* image (Dr. Jolly Jekyll) and the *negative image* (Hideous Homecoming Hyde). The conflict creates frustration followed by anxiety about homecomings, which is reinforced if the negative treatment is repeated.

Because he did not associate the punishment with the *act* of chewing up something, the next time he is left alone the puppy seeks out another book, or perhaps a shoe, and repeats the negative behavior. The cycle is repeated until both owner and dog have mixed emotions about each other. Their relationship is deteriorating. The owner may conclude that the punishment was not severe enough and so the correction was not permanent. So he intensifies it. The relationship erodes further as weeks go by. Enough of this cascading negative effect and the owner is ready to take drastic action.

Now highly sensitized to his owner's mood change, the maturing pup *feels something is wrong.* This is often reflected in new problems: submissive wetting when owner comes home or approaches the pup, off-schedule bowel movements or urination, and so on. The insecure puppy now seeks more favor when the owner is home and misses the owner more acutely when left alone. Frustration and anxiety build, fueling the isolation-related, tension-relieving misbehavior.

The unwitting owner originally may have thought the pup was "getting even" for being left alone, but now begins to wonder if the maturing dog is incorrigible. Outside help may be sought. Unless an enlightened behavioral consultant is available, advice from books or other people may find the puppies stuck into a cramped crate or cage all day, put out in the yard or garage, or with his mouth stuffed full of chewed debris and taped shut for hours. Too often puppies and older dogs go to the pound where they face a potential life-span of five to seven days.

This happens because the owner does not understand how canines think and is ignorant of the pup's needs.

Needs of Dogs

Daily life for a pet dog is vastly different from his wild cousins. When the wolf pack stirs at dawn, there is much **stretching**, and some **social touching** or brief eye contact as some members move away from the area to relieve themselves. If hungry, the pack usually behaves restlessly until the pack leader starts off for the area where prey may be found. On the other hand, the pet dog wakes to greet his people, who open doors to allow access to the toilet area. Then the dog eats breakfast. His survival does not require him to function as an important part of a cooperative group to hunt to find food. That need remains frustrated.

When the hungry wolf pack downs the prey, each individual eats according to his rank in the pecking order. This status is well defined and maintained through **rituals of dominance and submissive behavior.** There is seldom any serious challenge or fighting as this would endanger both the health and social fabric of the group, which is basically cooperative.

In the wolf pack there is time for **napping and play**. Evening finds them seeking high ground, sheltered from rain or snow by trees or brush, where their keen noses and ears can best detect possible danger. Sometimes a group howl and romping play are the order of the evening. When sleep overtakes them, wolves circle to bed down and make a nest. When they wake, they take long, striding stretches, often with their rear legs dragging behind. This probably gets tendons and muscles supple and ready for the day's activities. This stretching is also seen after daytime naps.

Meanwhile, the house pet is left to his own devices for up to ten hours while his owners go to work. If he is kept in a cage or crate, those beneficial long stretches are denied. Also, there is no daily group function to satisfy his social drives. When the owners do get home, the dog is usually ecstatic to see his group members. When he

Isolation fear.

acts hungry, his people serve him. They then play doorkeeper so he can get to the toilet area again. When the dog nudges for attention, he usually gets dutifully petted. It is no mystery how the average pet dog gets the idea that he is the leader of his owners.

It is also easy to understand how the dog gets frustrated when his owners go off and leave him behind. His automatic door openers and petting machines have abandoned him. Nothing frustrates leaders (human or canine types) more than being forsaken by their followers. *For this reason, when training or dealing with behavior problems with dogs, the first step toward correction is to convert the owners from their roles as servants and followers to that of leaders.*

Leadership is a social function. It does not result from simple training exercises. Every time a puppy or dog nudges for petting and receives it, the pet is exercising leadership. When he goes ahead of the owner from room to room or through doorways he is saying, "Me leader." The dog that is not led by his owners will attempt to become leader itself. To apply human leadership effectively, you must learn more about your dog's natural reactions, senses, and social development.

Up, Boy! Up on the table! He does it all the time at home. Up!Up!

Your Dog's Natural Reactions & Reflexes

The concept that thinking is composed of reflex actions (and reactions) within the brain's nerve networks and chemical content was a favorite theory of the Russian, Ivan Pavlov. Modern computer designers use models derived from such theories. However, computers are still relatively crude devices when compared to the capacity of the brains of humans and other animals to receive, classify, compile, retain and recall information, to initiate action or no action,

11

or develop emotional impressions about life's experiences. Even so, understanding what little is known about reflexes will help to provide a better understanding of how a dog thinks.

Reflexes

Reflexes are gifts from nature (inborn or unconditioned) or the result of experience (learned or conditioned). Without reflexes, we couldn't get up in the morning nor swallow food. It would require a textbook to describe all of the dog's reflexes, so I will mention only those that bear on training or on the development of problems and their corrections.

Conditioned versus Unconditioned Reflexes

Years ago, Pavlov put dogs on tables, harnessed them securely, and taught them various things, among which was to salivate when he rang a bell. The dogs quickly learned this trick because they were usually hungry when the experiments started and were given food shortly after the bell rang. Salivating for food is an unconditioned (not learned) reflex, while drooling for the bell is a conditioned (learned) reflex. Pavlov's studies helped to classify reflexes in a way that is useful in understanding dog problems.

Freedom Reflex versus Inhibition

Pavlov noticed that all the dogs struggled, some mildly, some wildly, when they were first put into a harness. So impressed was he about this reflex that he called it the "freedom reflex." The important thing about the strength of this reflex is that it relates directly to how excitable the dog is. Excitability is a condition Pavlov attributed to the whole nervous system, especially the brain. He measured it by testing how strongly dogs reacted to various stimuli. At the other end of the scale was how quickly dogs' nervous systems quit reacting to stimuli, which Pavlov called inhibition.

Though we may disagree with many of Pavlov's methods, one of which was creating grossly neurotic dogs, his studies did produce useful information. Here are some of Pavlov's helpful findings:

- Excitable dogs are easier to upset emotionally and make neurotic.

- Excitable dogs go crazy actively, outwardly — a condition called "mania."

- Dogs with "balanced" nervous systems are more difficult to unbalance emotionally.

- Inhibited dogs are more difficult to make neurotic.

- Inhibited dogs react inwardly when they are emotionally unbalanced and become "depressed."

Keep these principles in mind when you are selecting a pup. Consider which type does best in your particular environment. This will help you to avoid behavior problems. Pavlov and his followers also documented many important findings about how dogs learn. Here are two of them:

HOW DOGS LEARN

- It takes six weeks of regular training before a learned (conditioned) behavior tends to become permanent.

- Most dogs need to be taught in several different locations, with increasing distractions, before they can perform a task dependably. This explains why your dog will sit nicely for you at home or in the yard, but "goes deaf" when you get to the veterinarian's office. Don't blame the dog. Teach him to sit in different locations over a six-week period and you can solve the problem.

Defense Reflexes

Defense reflexes become evident when the dog perceives a threat to his well-being. It is important that you understand that humans and pets possess defensive behavior that will surface when faced with physical harm. This natural endowment is not a character flaw in man or animal. It is merely a fact of life. Faced with a threat, a dog will either fight, flee, or freeze. If you use physical punishment to correct undesirable behavior and your dog is a passive, freeze type, the mildest sign of a physical threat will probably get your point across. The flight-type dog will retreat, but might also bite if held or cornered for punishment. The fight-type may tolerate a certain amount of harsh treatment, but beware! Nature will win out. Eventually you may need to settle the issue with a club, or you may find yourself in

"Give her one tranquilizing tablet before guests arrive, two before riding in the car, and eight before she comes to me again."

the emergency ward for some expensive stitchery. Many fight-type dogs suppress their active-aggressive defense tendencies with the person who punishes them, but will not do so if someone else (often the child of the family), makes what the dog perceives as a menacing move. The result could be an injured child and the death of a pet dog, victimized by a sad combination of his basic nature and human misunderstanding.

Fortunately, there are alternatives to force and punishment. I have helped hundreds of owners with active defense-reflex (fight or flight) dogs achieve satisfying lives with never a sign of such misplaced aggression. We simply work with the causes and avoid punishing the symptoms.

Defensive Biting

Some dogs bite defensively when someone blows air into their ear. A dog will even bite a bicycle pump if it is used for this purpose. Sadly, many little human faces are scarred every year because children hug dogs around the neck and innocently exhale a gleeful puff into the pet's ear. Most dogs learn to inhibit this bite reflex, but, even so, the best policy is to train your child not to breathe into even the most docile dog's ear.

Anything that moves quickly into a dog's field of vision can also stimulate a defensive bite reflex. This accounts for most of the oral bee stings dogs suffer. It's the same reflex that causes a human baby to grab things that suddenly appear or adults to reflexively catch a ball tossed unexpectedly. Unfortunately, the dog's equipment for catching things is full of teeth! As a result, many well-meaning people get nipped when reaching to exchange a little affection with the new puppy. This can lead to severe punishment for the pup, unless the owner is enlightened.

Having used the simple defensive bite reflexes as an example, let's now consider the overall canine nervous system and see how it's wired for reflexes, both inborn and learned, and how a dog's general excitability (nervousness) affects behavior problems and their corrections.

The Orienting Reflex

The orienting reflex alerts your dog to changes in the environment. It is important to understand the kinds of things that trigger this reflex, what effect they have on the dog's mental processes, and how they can take part in causing or correcting behavioral problems.

Man, dogs, and other mammals share this lifesaving orienting reflex. It operates through our senses to let us know something outside, on, or even inside our bodies has changed. A simpler name for it is the "What's that?" reflex. The internal effect of this reflex is an extremely brief interruption of ongoing mental activity, plus, in the case of an outside-the-body change, attention (orienting) toward the source of the change, or stimulus. Without the orienting reflex we wouldn't notice dangerous things like approaching cars until we feel the crunch of a collision.

The mental process of locating and interpreting the nature of the stimulus immediately follows the orienting reflex so that we can make a decision whether to do something about it, such as put on the brakes to avoid an approaching car. The sensitivity of the orienting reflex depends on our degree of alertness. It is nearly dormant when we slumber, so a very strong stimulus is required to trigger it. On the other hand, when we are "wound up" even a very weak stimulus (someone lightly touching our shoulder) can startle us, and a strong stimulus can cause our hearts to skip a beat or two.

With their super keen senses, dogs are especially reactive to orienting reflexes. This provides us with a marvelous tool for teaching simple commands like come, sit, and stay without leashes or the need to touch the dogs. More important, though, is that the orienting reflex opens a virtual pathway to our dogs' emotions. This is because the ori-

The orienting reflex alerts the dog to life's hazards.

enting reflex is followed by other reflexes for locating, interpreting, and deciding what, if anything, to do or how to feel about the stimulus that started the whole chain of reactions. If we learn how to affect and change the way a dog feels about things, we'll have the secret to solving even severe problems. Let's take a case and see how it works.

You have a dog that shows extreme aggression toward visitors. One visitor has been bitten. We won't bother now to consider how this problem developed, only what you did to try to control the aggression. You answered the door and held the dog's collar, petting and speaking soothingly to reassure the dog. That didn't work. In fact it made things worse. So you tried negative feedback routines: you scolded, spanked, put the dog on a leash. The dog's ferocity grew wilder. Now, you put the dog out or in a separate room when folks come to call.

All these steps failed for the following reasons: petting and reassuring tones were interpreted by the dog as approval of his feelings of hostility and aggressive behavior, so things got worse due to positive reinforcement. Then, the heavy-handed stuff (a negative conditioning) failed because the dog associated the arrival of people with your disapproval. The ultimate negative conditioning was exclusion from the "pack." Soon the situation is so bad that your dog starts barking and charging the door when he hears footsteps out front, or when a car door slams, both signaling possible visitor arrivals. Worse, the dog now growls when you grab his collar to take him to the other room or outdoors. Now you're afraid you may get bitten!

The Interpretive Factor

So, now what can you do? I coined the phrase "interpretive factor" to define that instant following the orienting reflex when you can impress on the dog how to interpret (feel about) a stimulus. One way to use it follows.

Since your pet's nasty behavior is a result of his feelings of hostility, the solution lies in changing his emotional interpretation of the situation. This must start well before he is facing people at the door. Fortunately you have one vitally important emotional element in your favor. Your dog loves to play ball about as much as he hates the arrival of visitors. This will be important when using the orienting reflex and interpretive factor. Here is the sequence of events in a correctional "setup."

The chain of reconditioning the dog's emotional and behavioral reaction goes like this:

- Have an accomplice outside to start approaching the door.

- Footsteps occur; dog alerts; footsteps instantly stop.

- Instantly after dog alerts, you clap hands, bounce ball, happily move about and invite dog to play until he takes part.

(The hand-clap and ball-bounce cause a second orienting reflex, which interrupts the dog's initiation of hostility. The happy movement and upbeat invitation provide a new interpretive factor—one of happiness

The Jolly Routine

The above procedure is known as the "Jolly Routine." Use it to correct most of the serious emotionally based problems, including fearfulness. The Jolly Routine must be applied while gradually bringing the footsteps closer to the house, until the guests can arrive at the door and take part in the ball game.

> **Warning:** there is much more to correcting aggressive behavior than merely applying this Jolly Routine. First you need to gain a position of emotional leadership with your dog, to be described later. Otherwise you could be running around bouncing the ball while your dog is trying to tear the front door off its hinges!

The Jolly Routine.

The Chase Reflex

The chase reflex appears as soon as pups are able to move around on all fours. They pursue and pounce upon anything that moves fast. This is invaluable for developing prey-catching skills in the wild, but it gets exasperating when practiced on human ankles and clothing. It becomes genuinely vexing when it is triggered by bicycles, cars, and joggers. This predatory game-chasing reflex does not have an emotional base in most cases. However, it requires extra portions of patience, effort, and time to correct (See the Chasing Cars correction program).

The Resistance Reflex

Numerous reflexes combine to keep a dog's body in any particular position; standing, sitting, lying down, or in any stage of movement. One reflex that is useful with problem dogs and for teaching certain types of behavior is positive thigmotaxis. For clarity, we'll call it the

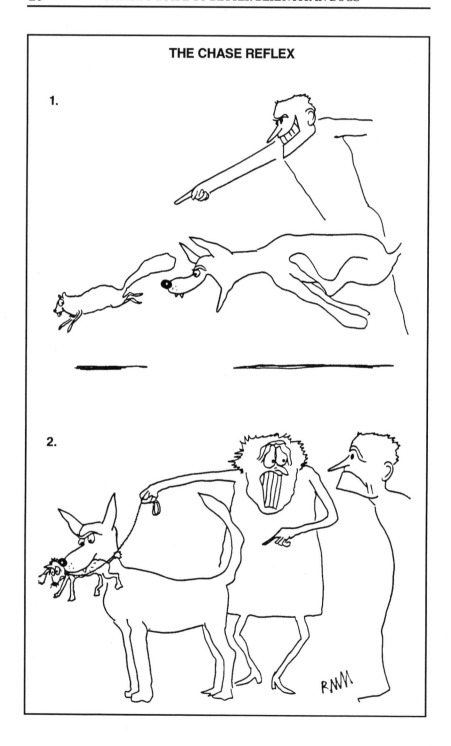

"resistance" reflex. You can test it in your dog by gently pressing against the side of his rump while he is standing. That pressure pushing back at you is positive thigmotaxis. If, instead of pushing back, the dog gives way, you have stimulated negative thigmotaxis—a rare response except in dogs with severely inhibited nervous systems or those suffering from isolation from normal social contacts during puppyhood. Understanding the push-back reflex helps avoid and solve some problems.

For instance, the best way to stop a pesky dog from **leaning** against you is not to push him away, which can stimulate a stronger lean by the dog. Rather, suddenly remove the part of your anatomy the dog is leaning on. This will upset the dog's balance and he will either collapse onto the floor with indignity or his righting reflex will jolt him upright. Doing this enough, with praise when the dog quits leaning, will solve the problem. Be sure to do this in several locations and every time the leaning occurs. One "unbalancing" lesson doesn't necessarily solve the problem.

This reflex is the main reason why dogs are great at pulling sleds or carts. Unfortunately, they can also become people-pullers. The sight of a person being hauled down the street by a dog is incredibly common and often comical. It is surprising how quickly most **leash strainers** can be permanently corrected in the early stages of their careers. Just start with a loose leash and turn and walk in the opposite direction, calling his name, every time the dog starts to pull you.

If we consider this reflex with the freedom reflex, it's easy to understand how tethers and tight leashes can cause frustration and aggression in dogs. In fact, for some dogs, fences alone create enough frustration to result in severe aggression toward people or other animals beyond reach.

Eating and Elimination Reflexes

At birth, puppies have reflexes that cause them to root toward warmth and to suckle on just about anything resembling a nipple. This and a swallowing reflex makes the newborns well-equipped to get nourishment, but nature neglected to give them a reflex to eliminate wastes. A human baby's full bladder sends a message to his urinary sphincter, and that muscle relaxes to relieve the pressure. Not so with newborn pups. The mother must lick their genitals and anus to stimulate elimination, otherwise they would die of blood poisoning due to blockage of urine flow from the kidneys. This quirk of nature, used properly, makes house training a puppy a simple matter compared to toilet training a child. The reflex to urinate or defecate can be absolutely predictable in pups and adult dogs. The program you will see later uses these principles as a vital link to quick, effective house-training.

Thus we see that a dog's reflexes are natural reactions to what he is sensing from the outside, as well as from the inside, of his body. These are significant differences between man and dog and understanding them will help immensely in understanding and correcting canine behavior.

How Your Dog Senses His World

If we don't understand that the dog sees, hears, smells, tastes, and touches the world differently than we do, it will be impossible to develop insight into his behavior. Without such insight our attempts to train, shape new behaviors, or change existing behavior are limited to outmoded carrot-and-stick techniques. It doesn't require a lot of study, but once we understand the dog's sensory system, a whole range of problems can be avoided and solved quickly and humanely.

Vision

Canine vision is poor compared to ours when it comes to color perception, or identifying shapes or details within a form (such as noses on faces), yet dogs can see things when we would swear it is totally dark. They can perceive movements so subtle that we'd swear there was none. Their wide-angle vision is twice that of ours, while their focus vision is narrower. Remember that nature equipped our pets to survive as predators and these variations make sense. A slight movement of a single blade of grass at gathering dusk is detected by the peripheral vision, causing eyes and head to turn almost to the exact spot where the field mouse moved. So begins the stalk for dinner.

This sensitivity to subtle movement helps explain how our pets often seem to know when we are about to get up to leave the house, get dinner ready, or go to bed. We unconsciously make minute movements before taking deliberate actions. Dogs are astute people watchers, using their extra keen visual talents to keep up with or, at times, ahead of us.

On the minus side, poor shape, form, and detail vision may cause some dogs to become uneasy and even to freak out when they see their owners for the first time wearing a hat, using crutches, carrying a pole, or approaching in semidarkness. This is why it's a wise policy to speak in an upbeat tone of voice to your dog (or a strange dog) in these circumstances.

Canine eyesight is poor when compared to humans.

If your dog's hair hangs over his eyes, cut it off or tie it up. Life down on the floor is tough enough without having to look at the world through a picket fence. This avoids visual surprises when people reach to pat or pick up the dog. Contrary to popular myth, "hairy-eyed" dogs do not go blind when their eyes are exposed to sunlight.

These are the important visual perception differences between humans and dogs. Later we'll look into some fascinating, helpful, and troublesome reflexes connected to vision.

Smell

You and I can't even imagine possessing an odor sensor capable of detecting a human body buried for days under a snow avalanche, or identifying a chemical diluted in a million parts of water. This exquisite sense makes an evening walk a veritable mental feast for our pets. Noses create problems, too. Dogs have a strong drive to investigate odors, especially if the smell is airborne. *Many runaway problems start because the pet is drawn by an enticing airborne scent.*

Dogs use this olfactory sense to identify people and animals who exude airborne chemicals from every pore and opening in their bodies. The chemicals that beget specific responses from kindred animals are

He probably smells your dog on you.

called pheromones. For example, a female dog about to come into heat emits messages that can attract male dogs from miles around. Most pet dogs are content to sniff people at a respectable distance for identity odors. However, if they move in close to someone's crotch for more detail, or jump up to gain access to life's very essence, our breath, they violate human values and find themselves in big trouble. Such offenders, if caught early enough in their careers, can be corrected by asking people to crouch down to greet the dog. After a few meetings with different people the dog is usually content to settle for less intimate introductions.

Hearing

Another canine sensory organ that dwarfs its human counterpart is hearing. A keen-eared person can't detect footsteps sixty feet away, but the dog hears the walker at least four times that distance. Don't be surprised when your dog gets excited before the family car rolls into the driveway or starts barking long before the doorbell rings. Most *dogs also seem able to hear selectively* among all sorts of sounds and detect those that are important to them. You'll see this when your dog alerts to something outdoors while the TV is blaring. Dogs can easily pick up ultrasonic frequencies at least twice as high as those we can hear. This is why silent dog whistles and other ultrasonic devices cause an orienting reflex in dogs. Most dogs do not find such sounds unpleasant unless they are extremely loud.

If you want to train a reliable watch dog, realize this exquisite sense and don't shush the dog when he barks at things you cannot hear. Instead, help him investigate by cautiously leading him toward the source of the sound. If he is some normal neighborhood sound, such as kids on skateboards, act nonchalant and show the dog there is nothing to get excited about. But, when unusual sounds occur (for example, have a friend softly jimmy at a door or window), lead the dog to the scene and get excited yourself. This will help him learn the difference between okay and not-okay noises, and avoid the racket of a dog that barks at everything.

Even though they possess such acute hearing, dogs are not particularly talented at discriminating between different qualities or characteristics of sounds, especially those of human language. This leads to many problems between you and your pet. We hear people with disobedient dogs say, "He understands every word I say, but he's just being stubborn!" This is not necessarily true. While dogs' hearing nerves connect with brain centers functionally akin to human sound centers,

Hi-fi hearing!

dogs do not develop anything like our language and speech centers. This may be because their voice boxes do not function like ours, and their tongues, lips, and mouths are not shaped properly for the kind of speech we develop.

One way to appreciate a dog's perception of our spoken language is to join a foreign language class that uses the conversational approach, rather than the reading method, and forbids students to use English in the classroom. A lot of pointing, touching, moving about, posturing, and facial expressions will be used before you learn to do the right things when the teacher looks at you and says: "Venay! Ah-say-yay-voo! Res-tay!" When you finally do get it, you know that when the teacher makes those sounds you're supposed to "Come, Sit, and Stay," in that order. You also appreciate how important the teacher's expressions of approval are, especially when you start to take the first step toward her in response to the sound "Venay." The expressions of approval (praise) let you know you are thinking about the right thing and motivate you to continue toward the teacher with enthusiasm. With such positive, socially rewarding systems, people learn basic commands in French almost as quickly as dogs learn them! The dog has an advantage with his extreme sensitivity to posture and movement cues and his positive responses to approval in the form of praise and petting.

Discriminating taste.

Taste

Dogs are not burdened with social values regarding what is or is not proper to put in their mouths, so just about anything that isn't burning gets tasted and often swallowed. This includes rotten meat, garbage, bugs, and that ultimate no-no, stools (not the kind you sit on)! Though furniture, shoes, clothing, carpets, and the like are also on some dogs' lists of edibles, these nonfood items satisfy a psychological rather than physical appetite. You need to recognize that a dog's sense of taste is probably as good as his sense of smell, and both can get a pet into trouble around the house.

Touch

Touch (tactile) senses play a vital role in understanding canine behavior problems. *Where* you touch a dog has basic meaning, but *how* you touch is important, too. Canine and human nervous systems are designed with one basic aim: propagation of the species. To propagate, we must survive; to survive we need to get water and food, and shelter, avoid crippling injury or being devoured by another meat eater, and to respond appropriately to sexual stimulation.

Let's consider this vital tactile sense and some basic reflexes necessary to survival and propagation as they lead to canine behavior problems. *An unexpected touch on the muzzle, head, neck, or body (especially from the withers to the base of the skull) triggers a brainstem reflex to bite.* From an evolutionary view this is important. In the wild, even an instant's hesitation between touch and defensive action, such as turning to see if friend or foe has pounced, might result in serious injury or an unpleasant trip as a lion's dinner.

Fortunately, nervous systems don't stop at the top of the spine with the brain stem. We have more elaborate brain centers that control (inhibit) such basic reflexes. Without these, neither dogs nor babies could be house-trained. Through gentle handling by people, dogs learn to control the primitive defensive bite reflex and usually respond affectionately when touched, except when they are drowsy or asleep. Hence the saying, "Let sleeping dogs lie," which unfortunately not all parents teach their children. *Such lack of training leads to thousands of dog bites every year* and a trip to the pound for many innocent animals.

Prolonged petting can send a mixed message.

Another defensive reflex is activated when the paws or legs of the dog are touched, especially unexpectedly. The response is to withdraw the limb. This seems logical for survival, since withdrawal ensures the dog's ability to take whatever action may be required, such as walking gingerly through a thorn patch.

These defensive reflexes occur in varying degrees in different dogs, even from the same litter of pups. Proper handling helps a pet learn to control them, but improper handling can actually strengthen them and confuse the dog. For instance, the touch-bite reflex makes clear how counterproductive it can be to swat a "mouthy" puppy across the nose. **A more sensible correction for the mouthy pup is to grab a paw to trigger the withdrawal reflex and praise the pup when he reacts.** This approach avoids the negative aspects that punishment can introduce to the relationship between owner and dog.

Courtship Behavior

People don't have a monopoly on foreplay. In dogs it is called courtship behavior, with much tail wagging, play invitations, and running together. There is also a great deal of touching, especially nosing around the ears and neck, leaning on one another, and sometimes putting the forepaws on the other's back. It is interesting that, within litters of puppies, almost every form of courtship behavior occurs as dominant behavior well before puberty. Some pups will respond to a human wrist or leg touching their throats or chests by firmly clasping it with their forelegs and performing vigorous pelvic thrusts. Most people won't tolerate this behavior, so they withdraw the arm or leg and either scold or punish the puppy. Fortunately, most dogs control their sex drives among a human family. *However, prolonged petting can send a mixed message and arouse sexual hormones so that the dog (male or female) experiences considerable frustration trying to keep their sexual drive under control.*

Pain

The sense of pain is closely associated with that of touch. Puppies raised in normal litters and transplanted to human families usually develop normal pain responses. But if a pup is raised in isolation from other living things, his pain perception, along with other capabilities, can be severely hampered. For instance, when first exposed to an open flame, isolation-raised puppies may continually stick their noses into it until blisters appear. They also fail to avoid objects moving toward them, even though such objects may cause pain.

Prolonged isolation beyond three or four months of age can cause pups to develop kennelosis. Like zombies, they barely react to anything. It is important to remember that dogs depend heavily on other living things for normal perceptive and emotional development. *In order to develop normally, puppies must have a great deal of social contact between the ages of six and twenty-six weeks.*

Direction

A dog's sense of direction may not be as sharp as a homing pigeon's, but it certainly beats man's. Well-confirmed stories abound of dogs leading their hopelessly befuddled owners safely home through blinding snowstorms. We do not know which sensory system makes such uncanny abilities possible, but it can be troublesome during **house-training**. Dogs must learn the route to their toilet area before they are dependably house-trained. If they have to move north from the food bowl, turn west around the corner, then south to the back door, west out the door, and then north to the toilet area, they are faced with a literal maze-learning problem. Since the first and final legs of the journey are northward, many unsupervised dogs take a directional shortcut and wind up relieving themselves close to the north wall, but inside the house. This is as close as they can get to the toilet area by using their "canine compass." **A route that takes a straight line from food bowl to toilet area is easier for a puppy to learn.**

Balance

The sense of balance keeps both people and dogs on their feet. Dogs can learn to walk tightropes and move on either front or rear legs, alien as these feats are to the way they are built. Balance is important in only one problem—car sickness. Even then the cause is more often emotional than physical. Balance can help prevent or correct the problem of getting up on furniture. **If a dog is never to be allowed on the furniture, just move the furniture back and forth to upset the dog's balance when he jumps up.** If you can do it so the dog doesn't realize you're the cause, so much the better. A few "unbalancing" sessions will usually create a dependable floor-model dog.

Extrasensory Perception

All animals have biological clocks, but pet dogs especially seem to have an uncanny sense of time: for example, when their owners should be getting up, going for regular walks, or eating, as well as leaving and homecoming. This sense has been scientifically demonstrated as accurate to within about thirty seconds in a twenty-four-hour period. This can be one of the causes for problems associated with a dog being left alone (often called separation anxiety) or an overly emotional homecoming.

Extrasensory abilities are baffling enough when they occur in people. In our nonverbal dogs they are even more confounding. Problems may or may not be definitely related to extrasensory perception (ESP), but there is some food for thought concerning the dog's ability to anticipate storms and earthquakes, as well as to detect people's emotional states.

Some dogs get restless and exhibit whining or pacing hours or even days before thunderstorms or earthquakes occur. It is theorized that they somehow sense changes in humidity, barometric pressure, or the positive-to-negative ratio of the air's ionization. Some dogs actually disappear well before clouds appear in the sky. My case files indicate that the more fearful and/or hysterical a dog gets when the storm hits, the better are his forecasting abilities. Correcting such dogs requires that their initial feelings of fear be dealt with. This may mean that corrective steps must start hours before the storm hits. *Effective correction of behavior problems deals primarily with a pet dog's emotional perception of situations. Once this emotional element is changed from negative to positive, the dog's behavior changes, often with no further effort on the owner's part.*

Telepathy

Over the years, I have seen demonstrations of a communication link between owners and their dogs that defy scientific explanation. For instance, a young couple was at odds over the idea of getting rid of their ten-month-old female Shih Tzu. The husband was speaking angrily about the dog and his persistent house-soiling. His wife was standing off to one side. The dog, sitting at her feet, could not see his mistress, whose cheeks were wet with tears. A moment later I noticed the Shih Tzu's eyes were watering.

In another case, after his owner's death a dog that was in our custody suddenly ripped up a favorite Mickey Mouse squeaky toy given to him as a puppy by the owner. The dog had never chewed the toy during the several months he'd had it. In fact, the dog carried the toy around during the day and took it to bed with him at night. We later learned that the time of the owner's burial two thousand miles away was the same time that the dog destroyed the toy.

A somewhat scientific test of telepathy follows. A dog and his female owner lived in a close, healthy relationship for several years. The two were placed in separate rooms that were insulated from each other in every way scientifically known. A burly man entered the owner's room and started menacing her. (She had not been forewarned of this part of the experiment.) The lady was terrified. At that instant, in the isolated room where he had formerly rested quietly, the dog became extremely nervous and upset, whining, pacing, and seeking a way out.

These and other less scientific telepathic experiences abound in dog lore. Speculation on how these occur ranges from "spiritual links," to undiscovered brain emanations that penetrate all known insulation methods and materials. *This element may help to account for many problems I have seen which seem to spontaneously correct themselves after owners, who have been thinking of getting rid of the dog, make a firm emotional commitment to keep the dog no matter what*

the consequences. Whatever the explanation, our dogs somehow sense our underlying emotional states. This rather mystical dimension is often the key to understanding and doing something about many behavior problems.

CANINE BEHAVIOR AND THE SENSES

Dogs are astute people watchers. They anticipate our actions by noticing minute, subconscious movements we make.

Because their shape, form and detail vision is poor, dogs become unseasy when they see us in unusual costume or posture. Speak to the dog in an upbeat tone at these times.

The dog's extraordinary sense of smell invites him to investigate. Many runaways are drawn by an enticing airborne scent.

Dogs also have an acute sense of hearing and are able to hear selectively to detect those sounds that are important to them. Dogs pick up much higher frequencies than humans can hear.

Dogs have difficulty distinquishing between different characteristics of the human language. We can help by giving posture and movement cues and by praising.

Both a dog's sense of taste and smell entice him in ways that can get him into trouble when he responds to them according to instict.

Touching the forepart of the body or the dog's head unexpectedly triggers biting. Touching the legs or feet unexpectedly causes withdrawal. Touching also stimulates the dog's sexual hormones.

Dogs should earn their petting.

Their keen sense of direction makes it easier to housetrain a dog if their toilet area is in a direct line from food bowl and door.

Dogs sense changes in weather and often get restless days before a major storm. Their biological clock tells them when it is time for their owners to leave or arrive home. Nervous or anxious behavior problems are often related to such events.

How Your Dog Communicates

$\mathbf{S}$tance and movement speak volumes compared to the noises dogs make at each other or to people, though each is important in various situations. A low growl may be a warning to knock off some disturbing activity, or it can be a non-threatening pleasure sound when an otoscope is stuck in the ear for veterinary inspection.

When the growl comes from a dog standing with tail and hackles raised, however, the unmistakable message is that a battle could be in the offing. Besides the usual dominant and submissive postures and movements, dogs develop other ways to show submission and happiness by tail wagging, general excitability, prancing, and even jumping up and down. All of these fundamentals of dog talk are characterized in the following series of insightful cartoons.

Reactions to Threat

A pup or an older dog may react to perceived threats to his well-being by acting submissively in an effort to convey the idea, "OK, I give up. Please don't hurt me." If we recognize this, we should further realize that *to press an already submitting dog with more severe threats or painful punishment is to change the rules of the canine dominance/submissive ritual.* This often creates enough perceived threat to cause the dog to react in his basic defensive nature. *The result may be a pet that becomes a submissive wetter, a runaway, a fear-biter, or a dangerous, aggressive beast.*

Eye Contact

People who stare at other people make them feel uncomfortable. This is true throughout the mammal world. Dogs are not exceptions. This sort of psychological, long-distance bullying can create problems in the basic relationships between owners and their dogs. Staring can also provoke a dog to bite when practiced with aggressive, strange dogs. *Eye contact threats invite hostility where friendliness ought to exist.*

RMM

FUNDAMENTAL DOG TALK

Dogs show submission and happiness by tail-wagging, excitability, prancing, and jumping up and down.

FUNDAMENTAL DOG TALK

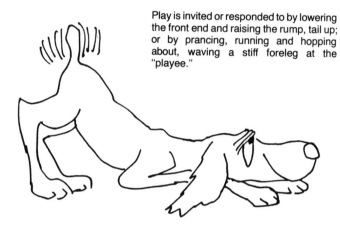

Play is invited or responded to by lowering the front end and raising the rump, tail up; or by prancing, running and hopping about, waving a stiff foreleg at the "playee."

FUNDAMENTAL DOG TALK

A frontal approach, with direct eye contact, tail and ears up, and hackles raised, is a sign that attack or a "bluff" is in the offing.

Circling another animal or person is dominant. Allowing it is somewhat submissive.

FUNDAMENTAL DOG TALK

A paw raised, with bent foreleg, is a submissive, friendly gesture.

FUNDAMENTAL DOG TALK

An absolutely still stance, with tail and ears up and the eyes rolled away, signals a readiness to fight, or that attack may be the next social gesture.

FUNDAMENTAL DOG TALK

A central position in a group can indicate a dog who either feels insecure, or "leader" of the group.

FUNDAMENTAL DOG TALK

Insecure and/or over-protective dogs often "cut out" a stranger by walking or running between them and the family.

FUNDAMENTAL DOG TALK

A playful nip from the rear can mean a friendly "How-dee-do," or a mild form of objection to something that is going on.

FUNDAMENTAL DOG TALK

Taking a hand, arm or leg and holding it in the mouth signals a bossy dog.

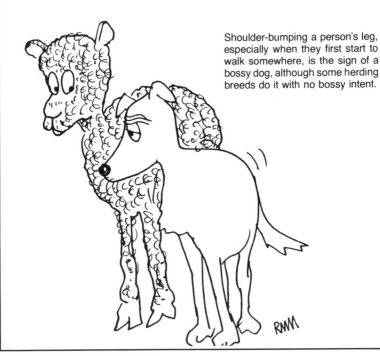

Shoulder-bumping a person's leg, especially when they first start to walk somewhere, is the sign of a bossy dog, although some herding breeds do it with no bossy intent.

FUNDAMENTAL DOG TALK

Direct eye contact, with or without expectant tail-wagging, but with no aggressive signs, says, "Pay attention to me!"

A nose "bunt" can signal a friendly greeting. It may also mean "Thank you" after you give water to a thirsty dog.

FUNDAMENTAL DOG TALK

Nudging with the muzzle or nose says "Pet me!"

Bossy dogs often take an outside position in a group, where they can "keep an eye" on everyone.

FUNDAMENTAL DOG TALK

"Come-hither" movements tell us to follow.

FUNDAMENTAL DOG TALK

Some pets show their teeth in a kind of snarling smile, especially when greeting people. (I call this a "snile," or "smarl.") It is usually shown by submissive types, and is often misunderstood as being aggressive.

A paw on the leg is generally a friendly invitation for petting or play, or means "Pay attention and await the next command!"

FUNDAMENTAL DOG TALK

Pet dogs adapt to and learn about human body language, too. If you crouch, especially sidewise toward a puppy or dog, they will usually approach in a friendly manner.

FUNDAMENTAL DOG TALK

When its owners stand or walk side-by-side with outsiders, most dogs interpret this as a friendly relationship.

FUNDAMENTAL DOG TALK

Face-to-face meetings between owners and outsiders may trigger aggression. This may be learned from witnessing family arguments, which are usually conducted from similar positions.

FUNDAMENTAL DOG TALK

When a stranger stands or sits *within* the family group, the dog may interpret it as pack-invasion, even when people are side-by-side.

FUNDAMENTAL DOG TALK

Standing stock still in the presence of an aggressive dog may trigger attack. It is better to stand sideways to the dog, leaning slightly away from it, and turning smoothly with it if it starts to circle. Avoid *locking* into direct eye-contact.

Social Development

All domestic puppies transfer their social tendencies from their own kind to the human pack. This is because of built-in reactions that appear shortly after birth. Some of them lead to problems, but they also can form the basis for many corrections.

Life in the Litter

Urination and Defecation

Unlike human babies, puppies do not arrive with an independent physical mechanism for urinating or defecating. If their dam did not roll the pups onto their sides or backs and lick their genitals and anuses to cause urination and defecation, they would soon die from the toxic effects of backed-up urine. After the roll-and-lick ritual, the good mother laps up the urine and eats the fecal material. This may seem disgusting, but healthy puppy waste is sterile, and this routine guarantees litter hygiene. As mentioned in chapter 2, this also creates a great mechanism for later house-training, since the little ones develop a reflex habit of evacuating their waste matter shortly after eating or drinking.

Submissive Signals

Another reflex response to the mother's licking occurs as she cleans up about the youngsters' faces and throats; they raise their forepaws as if trying to fend off the attacking tongue. As the mother persists, most pups give up the battle and draw their forelegs into the sides of their chests in a rather clasped knife position. Some even urinate. You can see both of these submissive responses in some adult dogs. A mild form occurs when a dog sits and raises a bent foreleg. In the litter situation, the pups experience their first exposure to dominance when the dam rolls them over for cleanup. Simultaneously the puppies, for the first time, display submission as a behavioral response.

Suckling and Swallowing Reflexes

Two other built-in reflexes are to suckle when hungry and to swallow when the suckled matter gets to a certain place in the mouth. Just like a human infant, a pup will try to get anything small enough into his mouth and give it a good working over. The reflex to root after anything warm and soft generally leads the pup to a nipple and nourishment. If he happens to get attached to a littermate's tail or foot, the mother will usually pull the errant puppy to the proper place. These rooting and suckling reflexes usually fade as the pups mature during the weaning stage. However, some adult dogs will suckle on blankets, and even their owners' clothing, when they feel emotionally insecure.

"Kissing" for Dinner

The weaning process begins about four weeks after birth. Many breeders force this process by taking the dam away from her litter. They usually provide a large tray of soft food so that puppies are able to waddle to dinner. Other litters are naturally weaned, and the mother will often start to regurgitate some of her own food, which the young gobble up. After a couple of these experiences, the pups begin to lick the dam around her mouth when she finishes her own meal, and she vomits in response. Many owners encourage puppies to lick their face, giving pats and praise. Later, when the maturing or adult dog jumps up to get a little "love and kisses," he gets scolded or punished. This inconsistency can lead to problems.

Chewing

When the puppies begin to eat more substantial food, they stop suckling and licking and begin lapping the food with their tongues or grabbing it in their jaws. In the wild, wolves and dogs start earning their dinner when they are between six and twelve weeks of age. They work for it in the sense that they must do a lot of ripping and chewing at prey animals killed by older pack members. This may serve a dual purpose: priming young noses and taste buds for their natural prey, while developing tremendously strong jaw muscles that eventually will crush many spines for survival. Pet puppies do not experience this chew-for-food stage, but usually gain strong jaws anyway chewing on toys. None of this toy chewing relates to filling their bellies, so this oral activity becomes a pastime, a sort of hobby. Being great fun, chewing often becomes generalized to the rest of the pup's environment. Almost anything becomes fair game—shoes, furniture, carpets. Fortunately, *chewing problems are basically tension-relieving* behav-

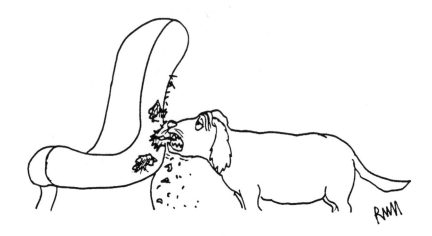

iors, so we can minimize these behaviors by removing the cause for the tension—that is, solving the frustration in the dog's life. Perhaps dog food may one day be sold in tough, edible containers that will keep pups and adult dogs busy for a half hour or more, chewing for their chow rather than gulping it down.

Following Behavior

A fascinating and useful behavior shows up as the pup develops vision sharp enough to see objects moving at a distance from the litter which the pup then follows. Just what is moving doesn't seem to matter; it can be a mechanical toy, littermate, his mother, or a person. Even if you isolate a puppy where he can't see any moving things until he is several months old, he tends to engage in this following response. This important tendency forms a basis for all his later bonds of social development. The response will also be an indispensable part of both the development and correction of behavior problems.

Social Competition: Dominance and Submission

Between four and seven weeks of age, puppies begin to sort things out socially within the litter. This starts with clumsy play fighting, which helps develop coordination and experience in determining who is strongest and/or more skilled in the physical arts, as well as who gets to the "dinner table" first. Some pups even try sexually mounting their mates with no obvious motive other than being bossy. Most of the biting during this stage is mild and rarely causes any evidence of pain. By the seventh week, however, things start getting serious. Nips get painful, growls become snarls, and fights produce winners and losers. Losers give up by running away (flight) or showing "freeze" behavior (passive defense response). Winners stalk around picking fights until they get whipped into submissive behavior themselves, meet their equal, and declare a truce, or wind up "top dog." Meanwhile, in the loser's bracket, further sorting out takes place to determine where on the social ladder each pup will rank.

It is important to understand that puppies, even the most submissive, are capable of acting dominantly, and that the most dominant of them will often display submissive behavior. The behavior chosen depends on the social circumstances. In an eight-puppy litter, the second ranked pup will act submissively to number 1 when he approaches dominantly. Later, number 2 will look like a number 1 as he approaches and dominates number 7 in the hierarchy. As the litter matures, these displays become very subtle signals. In the early stages, a dominant dog may have to pounce and pin an underling to prove its point. After a while, merely staring at a subordinate can cause him to lower his tail and head and look away, signaling submission. Another example occurs when the dominant pup approaches, tail up, ears forward, and places his muzzle over the subordinate's head or shoulders. The underling may stand still, lower his head and tail, and even growl as he raises his lips in a kind of smile. Boss pups learn to recognize and respect this growling and baring of fangs as part of the canine submissive ritual, so long as the other doesn't make a wrong move.

Submissive vs. dominant stances.

All this ritual keeps domestic puppies from injuring each other while among the litter, which is as far as most of them will mature together. In wolves and wild dogs, however, dominance and submission rituals will determine which animals eat first and get the best and most of the prey, as well as which ones breed. These rituals play important roles in the survival of the fittest and propagation of the species. Not so with our domestic pet dogs. Their matings are either accidental or based on physical conformation. Food is ample under noncompetitive conditions. While their wild cousins mature as cooperating members of functional packs, our pets are usually doomed to lifelong emotional and functional adolescence. We feed them when hungry, supply them with water, wash and groom them when dirty, walk or give outdoor access when needed, pet and stroke them when they nudge us (or just because we feel they are cute), and give medical attention when required. Since we wait on their every need and respond to nearly every whim, it is no wonder our puppies grow up feeling that *they* are the *leaders* in our relationships.

Learning to Fight

If pups are kept together as a litter through the ninth week or so, serious trouble can break out. Bully types become more so; midrankers vie with greater intensity, and all may turn on a particularly submissive puppy and injure or kill him. For these and other reasons yet to be mentioned I recommend that you obtain a new puppy between six and eight weeks of age. Observing the litter for about an hour before and during feeding time can be educational. If there is se-

A calm and confident owner begets a calm and confident dog.

rious **aggression** among puppies, and you dislike breaking up dog fights, it is a good idea to move on and look at another, more peaceful litter.

This seven-week principle for the transition from canine to human companionship does not mean a behavioral tragedy will occur should you get your puppy earlier or later. Fortunately, many breeders expose their litters to socialization before, during, and after the so-called optimum age. You should be able to easily recognize that this has been done when you observe the behavior in older litters.

The Dog in the Human Family

Imitative Behavior

The most important single social characteristic of a pet dog has a Greek tongue twister for a name: allelomimetic behavior, which literally means behavior that is "of one another imitative." "Allelo" comes from genetics, and mimetic was tacked on by pioneers studying genetics and behavior. The simplest form of this trait common to all social animals is when schools of fish or flocks of flying birds move and change direction as if they were one. Well-socialized litters show this trait when they all flock happily toward somebody entering the litter

"Has he been watching an awful lot of TV?"

area. On the other hand, unsocialized and poorly socialized litters may show fearful, extremely timid, or downright hostile reactions when people enter their domain. The important difference between dogs and other allelomimetic animals is that *dogs raised in human families will take their cues from people.*

Your pet dog reinforces your own emotional expressions of happiness and affection; he runs when you run, shows concern when you are distraught, and even shares many of your hostilities. Yet, ironically, the very things that create your close social bonds also lead to most of the behavior problems. *You cannot ignore the emotional aspect of your pet relationships and expect to understand canine behavior.* The causative approach to coping with or avoiding problem behavior depends on understanding it.

Investigation

An appealing but trouble-making behavior that begins blossoming at about six weeks of age is when the pup looks at, smells, paws at, chews, and tastes nearly everything in the environment. At the same age the vision of puppies is getting keener almost daily. So it is no wonder the puppy is always in "hot water" if left alone around the house. This intense investigating recedes with experience, but without proper guidance it can create major problems later. You should place things that might injure puppies out of reach, just as with a human infant, but allow as much investigation as possible.

If the pup starts toward a no-no, use a quick hand-clap and distraction toward another article or activity. If a puppy is alone, it is best to leave him in his regular sleeping area. This will usually cause him to sleep, since you are not there to stimulate activity. Canine play pens are sometimes helpful. They allow plenty of room for spontaneous bursts of activity and those long, crawling stretches after naps.

How Puppies Relate to Littermates vs People

The following incident illustrates some of the differences in how pups relate to littermates versus people. Years ago I did a demonstration on puppy selection for CBS-TV. We carefully observed a litter of seven-week-old Golden Retrievers, identifying the dominant litter boss and the lowest ranking pup.

As I entered the litter enclosure, the dominant pup led the group to jump up and greet me, while the most submissive, bottom-ranked pup (also the smallest) hung back timidly. I picked up the boss and gently carried him to an area away from the sight and sound of the litter, placed him on the ground, walked away, crouched down and beckoned to him, softly clapping my hands. He approached me cautiously, tail down. When he arrived, I gently rolled him onto his back and held him with one hand on his breastbone. He froze. When thirty seconds had passed, I released the puppy and placed him in a sitting position at my feet. The "boss dog" then proceeded to urinate on my shoe, much to the glee of the TV crew who were using a close-up lens! I picked up the puppy, praised and petted him during the trip back to the litter. When I placed him down back "home," he immediately started picking on the nearest litter mate.

I then took the submissive litter runt away for the same test. Tail up, she resisted my invitation to come, bit at my hand, flailed and scratched when I held her in the submissive roll-over position, and tried again to bite me when I put her in a sitting position to pet her.

This phenomenon, with few exceptions and variations, bears out the contention that *puppies do not necessarily perceive persons as they do other dogs, but react uniquely to each.* It also shows the difference between rituals of dominance and the ultimate defense reflexes to fight, take flight, or freeze.

Growing Up: Beyond the Litter

Between the time when the puppies leave the litter and the age of twelve weeks is a critical time for social and mental development. Much of the dog's adult behavior patterns are formed during this time. It is also a key period for the puppy to learn appropriate behavior and how to relate to his human family. Therefore, it is important that we understand as much as possible about the developmental stages of the puppy.

The Fear Period

As a pup approaches *ten weeks of age* there is a period wherein *certain events can produce lifelong fear responses.* Not only that, but other things associated with those fear-producing elements can become conditioned fear stimulators. You can use this to your advantage for teaching a pup to avoid venturing into streets on his own if you supervise the lesson carefully. However, it can also produce behavior problems based on unreasonable fears or phobias about being left alone.

For instance, a puppy yipped and wailed when left alone in the kitchen or laundry room on his first night in a new home during this fear period. His behavior was absolutely normal, but the new owner wanted to get some sleep. He had read somewhere that a "natural" punishment for puppies is to grab them by the scruff of the neck and shake them. The owner didn't recall (if the book or article even mentioned it) how hard to shake, what pup response to look for, what type of nervous system could or could not tolerate such punishment, or what type of defense reflexes might be most amenable to the shaking routine. So, he just started shaking, and the puppy started screaming bloody murder, another natural response. So he shook harder, which stimulated the pup to higher and louder wailing. Violent shaking finally stifled the puppy, who settled for soft whimpers and sought to get physically close to his new owner. The owner also read that he should praise the puppy for stopping unwanted behavior, so he picked up and cuddled the pup, told him what a good dog he was, placed him back in his box, closed the door and went to bed for an uninterrupted night's sleep.

If we hark back to the puppy's social, reflexive, and defensive properties, even ignoring the fear-response period, we can see the possible dangers in this type of approach. Some of the potential problems are obvious: submissive wetting in the presence of the man who punished him; extreme anxiety when left alone, resulting in tension-relieving, destructive chewing; difficulty in house-training; and biting the family children when they attempt to correct the dog later in life. These are not just possibilities, but are based on numerous case histories. More than one night's traumatic encounter is generally involved in producing adult fear-biters. However, this is a classic example of how early mismanagement sows the seeds for problems later.

Sexual Behavior Development Period

At about twelve weeks of age, puppies start going through puberty; they begin sexually **mounting** both animate and inanimate things. If there was ever an area of behavior where projecting human feelings to animals is valid, this is it. The sight of a puppy unabashedly humping away on a blanket or somebody's foot usually stimulates

"That's what I wanted to ask you about Doctor."

instant negative human feedback based on human moral standards of conduct. I have seen seriously aggressive male and female dogs, either neutered or intact, whose owners have either tolerated or encouraged their pet's misdirected amorous behavior. At the other extreme, overly harsh physical punishment can lead to the very same type of aggression problems. This paradox might be due to aggressive tendencies that develop at about the same age. Whatever may be the cause, **the best method for correction is to use the orienting reflex to interrupt the mental fix on the activity and instantly redirect the dog's attention to some play activity, such as chasing a ball.** This avoids the excesses of either permissiveness or punishment. When you use the distract-to-play routine, even the most persistent pups hold their sexual expressions in check in short order.

Sleep and Dreaming Patterns

From all outward appearances, puppies dream quite a bit. Just like people, their eyes move vigorously in a stage of sleep called Rapid Eye Movement (REM). If you wake a person every time his eyeballs start gyrating, you can cause all sorts of emotional and behavioral abnormalities, including signs of neurosis and psychosis, even hallucinations. *Depriving a pup or mature dog of his REM sleep has produced some bizarre canine behavior.*

In one case, the explanation given by the owners was that the pet seemed to be having terrible nightmares and that waking him seemed the humane thing to do. Back when I used to make house calls, I entered the apartment of a young couple who described their seven-

month-old female Fox Terrier as "irrepressibly unruly." Seeing no dog, I asked where she was.

"In the closet," came the unison reply. I suggested we let her out, but the lady said, "Before we do, I want you to know that if you can't help us we're going to have to get rid of her. John hasn't had a good night's rest in five months." John had been waking the dog every time he whined during a dream. In fact, John had been sleeping on the floor with Foxie for the previous three months!

When they opened the closet door, a canine behavioral cyclone hit the room. Foxie jumped up at us, raced around bumping into furniture and walls, barked incessantly, and was impossible to control. Before forty-five minutes passed, she wore herself out and went to sleep on the sofa beside me. Whispering, so as not to wake her, I advised John to rejoin his bride in bed at night and stay there. Even if Foxie's dream-state whimpering woke him, let her work it out herself. Five days later he phoned to say what a great dog they had. She even stopped chewing and barking when they left her alone.

The Aggressive Period

For most pups there is no need to learn the canine martial arts. However, at around thirteen weeks of age most of them act as if there were. Among other dogs they will engage in exhausting play-fighting sessions. Unless anger sets in, problems don't usually occur. However, **when play turns to anger, it is best to break it up by distracting the dogs without getting angry yourself.** Scolding or punishing either dog risks conveying the idea that you are taking sides in the dispute, which can increase the chances of far more serious fighting later.

Given no other animals on which to exercise their playful fighting tendencies, most puppies will either invite, or respond to, play-fighting with their "two-legged pack members." This can teach an unfortunate lesson; the pet learns to contest his people with physical force, which usually includes his jaws. Worse yet, if the puppy gets angry during the fracas, he has also learned to lose his temper with people and put real meaning into his bites. The possible consequences are clear; the human fighter either backs off or applies more force until the animal shows submission.

Canine horseplay has a role in wild packs, where it seems to help keep the group together. In many wild and domestic dog play-fights, the dominant animal rolls over, allowing a subordinate to take the dominant role. The reason for this exchange isn't clear. Bringing to

Discriminate between friend and foe.

mind the dog's various sensory capabilities and our limitations, people would probably make poor dog pack members, and trying to act like one isn't nearly as easy or effective as getting dogs to act like people.

Territorial and Pack Protection

Territorial and group defense behavior also start showing themselves in the early juvenile period. The dog that once welcomed strangers and known visitors gleefully now approaches them cautiously, sometimes aggressively, or even fearfully avoids them. These changes could be the result of the pup's improving vision that, at about this age, allows him to discriminate at a distance between family folks and outsiders. Many people who get dogs with protection in mind delight to see their pup bark and show aggression, so they encourage him wholeheartedly. This is as ill advised as is the practice of trying to reassure a puppy by petting him and saying things like, "It's OK, Tuffy." Both of these actions positively reinforce the pup's aggressive feelings and behavior. **Instead, he really needs to be taught to discriminate between friend and foe.**

People who do not want an aggressive defender also make a mistake when they scold or punish this behavior. This type of negative reinforcement can teach the pup to feel hostile toward visitors. Whatever the pup's behavior, **the best way to avoid problems and teach dependable watchdog behavior is to teach through leadership.** If it is a friend or non-threatening person approaching, we should show the pup this by approaching the person and standing alongside of or walking with him or her into the house, paying little or no attention to the dog. This allows the dog to interpret the situation as the owner feels about it. On the other hand, if we are unsure about the visitor's intentions, we should act that way. The pup will likely do the same, thereby learning from your example to recognize the contrast between situations calling for wariness or friendliness.

Territorial Marking

While on the subject of pack protection and territory, the need to brand things with urine or defecation rates some attention, although it develops later on, at five months of age or older. Objectively, domestic dogs don't need a wide hunting territory or to scent mark stations to scare off competing predators. They also do not need to roll in rotten carcasses or feces. Even without the need, most pet dogs seem to want to perform one or more of these practices. *It is as if the scent of another dog's urine, the approach of another animal, or a feeling of threat or insecurity about the pack or territory arouses the need to lay a brand on things.*

One way to *cause* problems such as chasing vehicles and people, dog and cat fighting, escaping, running away, excessive yard barking, household urine and/or defecation marking, and even aggression toward people, is to allow a dog to place his canine "Mark of Zorro" beyond his own legal territory. This creates a desire on the dog's part to return and freshen up his scent posts. Unless he can do this routinely, sometimes daily, he can become frustrated. If it is allowed too fre-

Mark of ownership.

quently, the dog may begin defending the territory aggressively. *Some dogs will even urinate on their own pack members when they feel a threat to their relationship. This is a way of saying, "You belong to me."* This, as well as leaving urine or feces on an owner's pillow or other belongings, may make a dog feel better, but people tend to regard it as insulting.

Vocal Behavior Development

Pups start making noises very shortly after they are born. These are associated with feeling hungry, hurt, too hot or cold, abandoned, or just content. As they start moving about, they add growling, snarling, yipping, and howling to their repertoire.

Barking starts at various ages, but when it first occurs, most pups appear perplexed, as if wondering where the noise came from. Depending upon the response, they will usually either bark a great deal or very little. For instance, if they are among a litter that has reasons for much barking, most of the individual pups will tend to be "barky."

In a human home, barky dogs can create problems. Also, quiet dogs can be made into barkers through innocent reinforcement by people. Howling as an expression of loneliness, or in response to the odor of a distant bitch in heat, is heard most often in breeds from the northern climes. However, once one dog in an area starts it, many others get the urge to join the chorus. **Correction or prevention involves distraction followed by soft-spoken direction to another activity.**

Leadership versus Obedience Development

With few exceptions, a problem dog and his owner are *competing for leadership.* Usually the dog is winning. The owner is backed into an emotional corner—too attached to take the dog to the pound or to a veterinarian for euthanasia. The thought of giving him away is unbearable. On an intellectual level, the owner has exhausted all possible means for correcting the delinquent and is reduced to seeking outside guidance. However, even though well in front in the leadership game, the dog acts as if he doesn't know it. He keeps the contest at a near-fever pitch, letting everyone know clearly from the moment they meet just who is in charge. Here are some examples of how they do this at our office.

When the family car stops safely in the consultation area, the door opens, and the dog bursts out ahead of everyone. Either that, or the owners must command him to "Stay" or physically hold him back. Good-natured, bossy dogs approach me and jump up to tell me to pet them. Nasty ones stalk around, hike a leg on my walnut tree, show me some raised hackles, circle me, or outright charge me to say I should not interfere with their "boss" position. When the owners and I head for the office door, guess who's there first? If the owner opens it, the dog barges through. To illustrate further for the owner, once inside, I ask the owners to get up as if to leave. No degree of human speed can beat Bowser to the door. It requires another command or some unreasonable physical force if the owner is going to score any points in this part of the leadership game. I see this so often, with nearly all problem dogs, that it is almost totally predictable. I see it in relationships where the dog was extremely submissive to the owner, and others where the dog attacked an owner for simply using a threatening tone of voice. Just who is *physically* dominant does not seem to be the deciding factor in most dog behavior problems. Rather, it is the dog that thinks or feels he is leader in the relationship that decides the issue.

Unfortunately, *when the pet dog assumes the burden of leadership, he must inevitably meet with frustration and suffer the anxieties and tensions that follow.* Why? Pet dogs spend most of the time with their people when the folks are home. They use their communication skills to tell the family when to feed them, when to open doors for them, when to take them for walks (as well as which direction to

walk), when to play with them, when to pet them, and sometimes even when to get up in the morning. These are the functions of a leader—letting people know how they are supposed to behave, not through a master/slave approach, but through canine language that most people find endearing.

The time comes when the leader dog, feeling responsible for directing the pack members, gets abandoned by his people as they go to work or have an evening out. Or the dog's subordinates act as if they should be directing things, such as when visitors arrive, that first time at obedience class, or at the veterinarian's clinic. Then, *as owners try to change the rules of the game, frustration sets in,* the contest usually intensifies, often gets physically rougher, and feelings are hurt on both sides. What might have started out to be an ideal relationship begins to fall apart. The dogs are suffering from the frustrated leadership syndrome, and so they react in ways that relieve their tensions, at least temporarily.

These dog behavior problems—destructive chewing, barking, biting, and so forth—in reality are just symptoms of that leadership struggle with the owners in daily life. At this point, many owners consider training the dog. While this seems logical, it does not get to the cause of the problem—the frustration the dog is feeling.

"So that night, after you ordered no more table scraps, we were eating a steak dinner and Flash sat up and begged, and I said, 'No, Flash. . . .'"

Puppy Training

Wild and domestic dogs put stock in ritual. Wolves ritualize their dominant and subordinate relationships with displays instead of going through the physical hassle of proving things with a fight all the time. So do domestic dogs. Obedience classes can be invaluable in this respect, particularly if a puppy is taught without a leash to follow his owners, come to them when called, sit when asked (and not get up until given permission), and to stay. An obedience class is a logical place to learn to get along with life on the end of a leash, especially if puppy classes are available.

Emotional Development

We will also concentrate on puppy learning. Training involves our conscious efforts toward teaching. However, *your puppy will learn his most important lessons when you are not deliberately training him.* These lessons revolve around the pup's emotional reactions to life's new experiences.

For example, the pup's first visit to your veterinarian helps shape lifelong responses to treatment. If he whimpers or cries when vaccinated and you act overly sympathetic or upset, *the puppy will get an emotional message* that there really is something to be upset about. On the other hand, if you are calm and happy, the pup will minimize his own behavior and follow your emotional example. This tendency holds true especially when the puppy is between five and thirteen weeks of age. It is vitally important that you expose your puppy to all sorts of people, babies, and other animals during this period so that he will develop a healthy personality. If you take the responsibility for emotionally guiding your puppy, you will help him grow into a well-balanced adult pet.

For instance, when you have to leave your puppy alone and you express concern while leaving, the pup will feel upset because you are upset. While he is alone, the emotional tension builds and problem behavior such as yelping, chewing, or house soiling may occur.

There are often a number of powerful daily rituals between dogs and owners. One of these is the "Dog nudges, owner pets" routine. When you consult the actual correctional programs later, you will no-

tice that nearly all of them take advantage of this ritual. However, they require that this problem-producing ritual sequence undergoes a major alteration, as follows:

"Dog nudges; owner pleasantly asks for some simple function (such as sit); dog sits and owner pets." Some very bossy dogs seem surprised when asked to **earn praise and petting**. Some even refuse to comply, move away and whine or bark in protest. Others go away or lie down and sulk, as a child denied a dish of ice cream. However, pouting is effective self-therapy. So in either case, if you ignore the behavior, the dog soon returns and gets the message that there really is no free lunch and the group has a new leader!

Name Recognition

Out of all the words your dog hears you utter daily, how is he to learn that any particular word is meant for him? The answer is simple: Just say the pet's name before any command word! For example, you name your puppy "Skip." What should "Skip" mean to him? It should mean "Pay attention to me because I am about to say something important to you."

However, if we chat with another person about what Skip did today, the pup soon requires that we change our tone or volume to gain his attention. Here is a tip that can guarantee lifelong instant response by your dog to his name: **Use a nickname when you are talking *about* your puppy, and use his real name when talking *to* him.**

Leader or Follower?

As important as emotional development is, a pup also needs to learn simple commands like come, sit, and stay, if only for his own safety. All dogs are capable of either leading or following. Leader pups become extremely frustrated when they cannot open doors, get their own food, and so forth. A follower is usually a happier dog because it accepts his people's directions.

Test your puppy to see whether he is a leader or follower type. Take him to an open area and walk away from him. Chances are he will follow you. If he does, say "Good dog" and crouch down to attract him to you. If he does not follow you, try running away from him and crouch to praise he if he starts toward you. Try to perform this exercise daily in all sorts of situations from the time the puppy is able to walk.

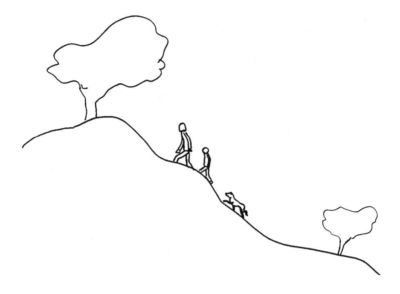

If the puppy does not follow and actually resists following, the following ritual can help achieve a better follower. Gently roll the pup on his back, holding him in that position with one hand on his chest. The puppy may struggle, cry, and otherwise resist the restraint. Calmly persist until the pup quiets down and remains still for a moment. When this happens, release him and give lots of praise and petting. The puppy will soon accept and even begin to enjoy the submissive position. Furthermore, you may notice that he will start following you when you take him out for open air exercise. This roll over is not recommended for pups older than four months.

Teaching the Commands

Many dogs with serious behavior problems are great performers in obedience class. Many are also washouts. In either case, **a simple, daily, off-leash ritual in the house in the morning can be extremely helpful.** It should be quick and intense, no longer than about three minutes. It need not involve more than calling the pup or older dog to come, sit and stay. Instant praise for each response and a few seconds' affectionate petting when he's finished are all that is required. What does this accomplish? A few minutes of intense "I'm leading, you're responding" helps to reaffirm the leader-follower relationship. It gives the animal a sense of having functioned and achieved all of his leader's approval. Every person in the family who is old enough to handle the dog should conduct the simple exercise. I have never seen it correct a behavior problem on its own, but as part of a larger, total program, it has been most helpful.

Teaching Come

Now let us teach come. Take your pup to an area that is fairly open, but free of strong distractions. Go to the center of the area and watch the puppy closely. The instant he takes his eyes off you, call, "Skip, Come!" Immediately crouch down, turn sideways to the puppy, clap your hands, and gleefully praise, "Good dog, Good dog, Good dog!" Keep up the praise and clapping until Skip comes all the way to you. Pet sincerely but briefly, then stand up and step away *behind* the puppy.

If his attention does not stay on you, instantly call, "Skip, Come," again and repeat the entire procedure. If Skip gets distracted, repeat the call and the praising-crouching procedure.

Continue until Skip will not leave you no matter where you walk. Then stop that teaching session. Do not hold another for at least two and one-half hours, otherwise you will be overdoing it.

For the second and following sessions, either create more distractions in the first area or go to a new area.

Hold three daily session at the most for six weeks. In between do not use "Skip, Come!" unless a panic situation arises wherein life, limb, or property may be in danger. In less serious instances when you

command, and to use it then might wear out the effectiveness of the full command.

Teaching Sit

Sit is the simplest thing to teach a pup. The difficult idea to get across is when to quit sitting! In other words, now that Skip is sitting, how long should he remain so? To communicate the total idea that Sit means to sit until I give you permission to get up, proceed by gradually lengthening the duration of the sit.

To achieve the sit portion of the command, first call, "Skip, Come!" using the full panic command in an undistracting area. When Skip arrives, pet and praise, keeping your left side toward the pup. Then, as you rise to stand, take your left or right hand and stroke under his chin upward to a spot over his head, so Skip must look upward and backward to keep watching that hand. As you do this, say "Skip, Sit."

Praise instantly if Skip keeps looking up at your hand. Lean a bit backward yourself, but do not loom over the dog. If Skip does not sit

down, merely repeat "Skip, Sit" and again make the over-the-head movement with your hand. The instant he sits, lean down and pet on the chest and throat, praising verbally as you do.

After about five seconds of sit, say "Free" and step away from Skip to communicate that he can now move out of the sitting position. Crouch down and praise and then keep repeating the entire procedure until sit is achieved on the first command. In this first session ask only for five seconds in the sit. In the next, try for ten seconds and keep doubling it until you have reached approximately five minutes.

If the puppy **starts to lie down** by your side after longer times have been achieved, do not correct or reprimand at this stage in the process. Remember, first he is learning to sit and remain in that place for some time.

Once sitting for five minutes has been achieved, you may then correct the lying-down behavior by using your hand movement to counter it the instant Skip shows a sign of beginning to lie down. Verbally praise the puppy when he corrects himself, which will be very quickly if you use this method.

Teaching Stay

Once again using movement as the communicator, begin work in nondistracting surroundings with "Skip, Come," "Skip, Sit." Then say

"Stay" as you abruptly bring your left palm from a position about a foot in front of the pup's nose to a spot about one inch from his nose. Stop your hand abruptly.

As he stops, step forward with your right foot (with the pup at your left side, the right foot is less apt to draw Skip forward) and face the puppy. Now you are confronting each other. This tends to keep Skip frozen in this sit-stay. Remain out front for only five seconds and then pivot back to Skip's side. Then, step forward with your left foot and say "OK" and release.

Just as with come and sit, proceed to teach in easy steps with minimum distractions at first, then progress to working in different areas and with greater distractions over a period of six weeks.

If Skip **starts to break** the sit-stay, avoid harsh corrections or manhandling. Just rush back to the exact spot Skip started the sit-stay; call him back and start over. Avoid punishment and negatives to retain your position of positive leadership.

WHAT CAUSES A DOG TO MISBEHAVE?

How People and the Environment Create Behavior Problems

Unfortunately, a book cannot consult with you and say exactly how you or your environment might be creating your dog's behavior problem. The following thumbnail sketches may, however, be useful in identifying some of these factors. With what you have learned about your dog's reactions, senses, social development, and ways of communicating in Part I of this book, you should be able to identify the causes for your problem, make various adjustments to your environment, select the appropriate correction program, and start on your way to an effective, humane solution.

The Human Element

These profiles of problem people and environments are deliberately exaggerated for dramatic effect. The cartoon humor may help you see more clearly into your situation. I am pictured perfectly as the Domineering-Physical-Verbal type. You may find yourself somewhere, too.

Name-Droppers

Name-Droppers sit around and talk a lot about their dogs, using the pet's name. Then they claim the animal ignores them when they use the same name to get his attention. No wonder. They "trained" the nonresponse. These folks benefit if they give the dog two names; a new one to use for talking about him, and the old one to be used only when speaking to the dog. **Use of the dog's own name should be followed by praise and petting, and used before feeding, and in various other pleasant situations.** Excellent, revitalized response is usually seen within a day.

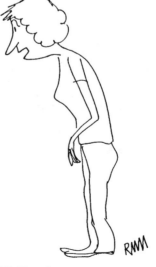

"Sit, Tippy."

"Down!"

Yo-Yo Makers

Yo-Yo Makers shout "Down!" while quickly raising their hands up away from the dog, which signals up. When Yo-Yo Makers learn to crouch down or reach down to pet the dog before he jumps, most jumping problems are resolved.

Back-Talkers

Back-Talkers usually put the dog's name after a command word (e.g., "Sit, Tippy"), rather than before it, which would let the dog know they are about to command him. When they realize that dogs do not hear backward, they turn things around and begin communicating effectively.

Pointers

Pointers stand rigidly upright with a demanding forefinger aimed at a spot by their side or feet, telling the dog to come. This body language actually communicates, "Stay still, like I am." Worse yet, they may send a message of aggressiveness and/or impending punishment.

The Whirling Dervish!

Pointers are generally amazed at how quickly their pets learn to come when they crouch, clap, and praise.

Whirling Dervishes

Nearly always late leaving for work, Whirling Dervishes race around the house getting ready, winding up their pet's misbehavioral mainspring. When they suddenly disappear, the dog is left to unwind itself without supervision. Many of them chew, bark, or dig at furniture or carpets. Setting the alarm clock five minutes earlier than usual and getting up when it goes off can help correct the dervish situation.

Neat-Freaks

Neat-Freaks make sure that everything is in its proper place, usually just before leaving the house. They go around adjusting throw pillows, and moving books, while the ever-watchful dog takes careful note. When left alone, *the pet mimics the behavior,* continuing the chore. Finding the owner's fresh scent on forbidden articles often makes them too irresistible not to chew on. To solve this problem, most Neat-Freaks have to break their own habits.

The Domineering Physical type.

Domineering–Physical

These types are hands-on people. They push down on their pet's rump, even when the dog knows the word sit. They don't often praise, either. They are also usually Pointers (the human type). This human behavior is usually motivated by the "me master, you slave" attitude. They often become excellent with dogs when they learn to use non-physical treatment. Once enlightened, they often ask, "Does this work with kids, too?"

Domineering–Vocal

The drill-sergeant syndrome is found in people with all sorts of personalities. It comes about most often through failure to reinforce the dog's desirable responses with liberal praise and some quick petting.

Sweet-Talk/Strokers

These attempt to gain the pet's loyalty and obedience through sweet talk and prolonged petting, usually called "fondling." This can create several reactions in the dog, from a desire to mount the owner, to a serious overdependency. Then, when the owner scolds the mounting, or leaves the pet alone, he becomes frustrated and anxiety sets in. Misbehavior follows.

Once these owners appreciate that *sympathetic tones and prolonged petting "spoil" the dog,* a more matter-of-fact tone is usually adopted and the "no free lunch," earned praise, quick pat technique helps solve the overdependency problem.

Permissives

These want their dogs affection and often give in. They allow things like getting up on the furniture, but don't allow it when guests visit, at which time the pet is scolded or punished. The inconsistency of the relationship frustrates the dog and leads to problems. Depending on the type of dog, the problems range from submissive wetting to viciousness toward the owners and/or guests.

Most permissive owners are very pleasant and easy to get along with among people but often complain privately that others take advantage of their good nature, as do their dogs! After seeing the benefits of using good-natured, but consistent, guidance with their dogs, these owners tell me they have even started saying "No" to unreasonable requests from their family and friends!

Ambivalent Owners

These people suffer from the classic love-hate relationship. That is, they love the dog but hate his behavior. Most are considering getting rid of the pet but say that they "want to do everything possible to solve the problem" before making that fateful decision. Ambivalent types need to realize that *dogs sense when their owners are not committed to keeping them no matter what*. When this commitment is made, the dog's behavior usually starts improving immediately and total correction follows quickly.

"Paranoid" Pet People

I put "Paranoid" in quotes because it is used here in a lighthearted and inaccurate way. But I have seen pet owners who would swear on the Bible that their dog or cat has it in for them. Most often the pet is seen as getting even or punishing the owner. If spiteful behavior does exist in pets, it must have been learned from people, because wild dogs do not display it. The bad behavior is just another way to release tensions caused by some frustration in their relationship. The solution is to change the supposedly spiteful behavior by removing its cause.

Common-Sense Owners

Common sense leads to sayings like "What goes up must come down." However, new information calls for a closer look at old ideas, since we now know that what goes up may never descend—at least to where it started from. In the world of dog behavior problems there are all sorts of corrections that appear to make common sense. Most of these concern doing something to the dog. For instance, it makes some sort of sense that if you fill a freshly dug hole in the yard with water and then stuff your canine excavator's head into it until he almost passes out, the dog will avoid digging in the area. As a matter of fact, most dogs actually will avoid digging there again. Even more predictably, however, the dog will find somewhere else in the yard to dig. So instead of the problem being solved, it spreads as the dog continues trying to work off that tension.

Another "logical" solution from a Common-Sense owner's point of view concerns the dog's practice of chewing up pillows and the like. This one says that if you stuff the chewed up material in the dog's mouth, tape the mouth shut, and leave it for some time, the dog will not chew that material anymore. This is sensible if you want your dog to avoid things that are already chewed up, such as tattered pillows. However, a little more common sense might bring one to the conclusion that unchewed pillows is what the dog ought to avoid. In the meantime, applying these seemingly logical techniques tears at the fabric of an already stressed relationship between owners and dogs. Frustration mounts, anxieties and tensions become stronger, and problems get worse. Too often, logical owners conclude there is something abnormal about the pet, and get rid of him.

Naive Owners

Naive types have never owned a pet before and usually select one that fits their preformed ideas about how a dog ought to look and behave. When the animal doesn't fit the notion, the owners usually follow everybody's advice, at least for a day or two. They are great book buyers, too. Let's hope this one helps!

Experimenters

These are usually recently married and want to use the pet, generally a dog, as a test animal on which to practice parenting. The trouble with this is that puppies mature to the juvenile level so quickly that the "parents" usually cannot make adjustments in their areas of disagreement between themselves before serious problems start to occur. The best advice for experimenter types is to raise dogs as pets and raise children as children.

Model-Buyers

They are not necessarily naive, but they obtain dogs with the misconception that certain breeds always behave in the same way. This myth is roundly supported and propagated by many dog breeders and the media, especially movies. When the behavior doesn't fit the myth, some Model-Buyers return the dog to the breeder for a trade-in. Some breeders actually take trade-ins.

It is important that Model-Buyers understand that each dog's behavioral development depends a great deal on the owner.

The Jekyll and Hyde Syndrome

We all have our ups and downs. The Jekylls and Hydes show their effects to their dog with gusto. They often leave their problem dog in the morning with apologies and words of consolation usually based on feelings of guilt. This convinces the dog that there really is something wrong with being alone, so he gets anxious and tense. Then, off to work goes kindly Dr. Jekyll. When Jekyll returns home and finds the dog has misbehaved, the diabolical Mr. (Mrs. or Ms.) Hyde roars into action. Ranting, raving, scolding and/or punishing, now convince the

"Bye, Bruno, poor lonesome boy! Be good, Bruno, baby! Daddy see you tonight."

"So,! You've been bad again, Bruno!"

pet that homecomings are also something to worry about. Thereafter, the specter of Hyde's arrival creates enough anxiety for some more tension-relieving misbehavior.

Jekylls and Hydes usually change their behavior when they *understand facts about the dog's biological clock, his inability to associate previous misbehavior with delayed punishment, and the need for consistency in human behavior to provide the reliable leadership dogs need.*

Problem Environments

Problem Children

Most kids get along well with dogs when the parents provide gentle and enlightened guidance to both. However, when emotional and/or physical parental excesses take place, children and dogs both tend to react according to the "Be-like, act-like" (allelomimetic) principle mentioned earlier. For instance, if an owner gets angry and scolds or punishes a child quite often, the dog may start getting edgy when the youngster is around him. On the other hand, if they do the same to the dog, the child may start trying to play the role of punisher and get into trouble when the pet defends himself. If owners have family

TABLE 8-1. CHILDREN'S ROLES IN DOG BEHAVIOR PROBLEMS

Child Behavior	*Dog Response*
Pulling ears, tail, hair; sticking fingers in ears, eyes	Growling, snapping, biting
Hitting with hands or objects	Growling, snapping, biting submissive wetting in pups
Teasing with toys, food; staring, wrestling to the point of anger or rage	Biting, viciousness
Encouraging aggressiveness toward outsiders, other dogs	Biting, viciousness, chasing, dog-fighting, cat killing, killing birds, escaping, barking
Tidbitting with food	Begging, overprotectiveness of food, food-stealing
Playing tug-of-war	Biting, stealing things, chewing
Screaming and/or running	Biting, jumping, chasing
Scolding, punishing	Growling, biting
Being unruly	Being unruly
Inter-child fighting	Aggressiveness, biting, over-excitability
Too much petting	Mounting, aggressiveness, males urinating in house, biting other children

problems, the best action is to seek some competent guidance about it while working on the pet's problems.

With that said, there are still some things children do with dogs that can be the basis for mild or serious problems. Table 8-1 lists them. Be sure to keep the "Be-like, act-like" principle in mind while handling them.

My Dog–Your Dog Jealousy

A young married couple had a two-year-old, spayed Doberman with a chewing problem. I always ask clients why they select a certain breed of dog. The answer in this case was protection, which in these times is not unreasonable. The next question was why they got a female. The wife answered, "Oh, Bob picked her, probably because he knew that females like men better than women." Bob's rejoinder was immediate: "Not at all, Martha. I didn't get a male because I was sure you'd spoil him so much that he'd get overprotective of you!" "Well," Martha retorted with a withering stare at Bob, "She's your dog and it's your problem. I just came to this consultation because Bill said it would be helpful." If looks could kill, Bob would have been on his way to the mortuary. Meanwhile the dog began to whine.

I broke the mood, saying, "Since you've put your finger on the problem, let's figure out how to resolve it." With that, we were on our way to working with the "green monster syndrome," jealousy, which is often involved in problems. Jealousy over a dog is tough to work out,

since it is usually never expressed openly. Bob and Martha were exceptions to the rule. There is a way to bring the green monster out and slay it: Talk about it. But, if things get too hot emotionally, spare the dog. Go out to dinner or take a walk. Discuss hang-ups and agree on how to conduct whatever correction program fits the problem.

War Zones

These are households with two or more people and one or more dogs. The people spend a goodly amount of time firing verbal blasts at one another. These are either low-level holding actions, or full-scale attacks. They are sometimes accompanied by hand-to-hand combat, especially if teenage children are involved. Not all war zones are so evident. Some involve intermittent sniping, which takes the form of verbal zingers, usually aimed at the ego structure of the enemy. In either case, the problem-dog gets into the action one way or another: directly by joining the combat forces through aggressiveness or barking; or indirectly, in ways that vary from chewing to self-mutilation. War zones often require professional mediation but at least warrant a stable truce if the dog's problem is going to be solved.

Hermitages

Hermitages are at the opposite extreme from war zones. Usually occupied by one person and one dog, they can also have several of each. The people don't like outsiders, so the dog never, never gets to find out about them, except for trips to the veterinarian. In extreme cases, house-call veterinarians are used. Under such conditions, active, socially outgoing dogs can develop problems ranging from unruliness to aggressiveness. Calm, submissive types usually do better.

The Fortress Syndrome

The Fortress Syndrome is seen in households where *people distrust nearly everyone.* Owners peek out windows when cars pass or pull up. Every noise is investigated to see if prowlers might be in the yard, or out in the hall if the fortress is an apartment. Fortresses are often established as a reasonable response in high-crime areas. Dogs residing in fortresses can acquire problems of all sorts, but usually bark too much or become overaggressive.

How Health and Nutrition Affect Your Dog

Regular veterinary checkups and routine inoculations may seem to have nothing to do with the behavior of your pet, but dogs and other pets are more likely to develop behavior problems when they have a physical problem. When you feel a nagging pain in your tooth, ear, or stomach, you have the freedom to visit your dentist, otologist, or general physician. Not so with your pet. Unless that nagging pain is accompanied by a swelling or eruption, or hurts so much that the animal cries out, he is doomed to suffer in silence.

Health

Animals can react to physical problems very much like people. They can get irritable and become withdrawn or easily excitable, but they also may start to urinate too much, over or undereat, chew themselves or other things, bark excessively, or exhibit other unusual behavior. The only defense against the behavioral side effects of less-than-good health is a regular examination by the one individual with the qualifications to declare an animal fit—your veterinarian.

During the years I operated a full-time behavioral consulting service for pet owners, it was a policy that clients have their pets examined before starting any course of correction for a problem. This policy sprang from hard experience, not accident. A case illustrates the point.

Hyperkinesis in Dogs

Many clients brought dogs to me that did not appear able to settle down, along with other complaints ranging from biting to house-training problems. Dealing with the main complaint was hopeless. The dogs, for the most part, were absolutely uncontrollable. Not only were the clients and I unable to control them; the dogs themselves seemed incapable of any self-control. Their every waking hour was spent in activity.

During this time, some extremely important work was being done at Ohio State University's department of biopsychiatry by Samuel Corson, who was working with dogs showing hyperactivity. Through proper veterinary examination, more than 3 percent of my clients' pets were discovered to be hyperkinetic, similar to hyperkinesis in children. After proper medication with *Ritalin* or dextroamphetamine, the behavior of these dogs changed dramatically, making them easy to handle and a pleasure to live with. Where many clients have considered euthanasia, even if privately and with remorse, they instead gained what they called literally "new dogs."

Physical Ailments and Behavior

The results of proper diagnosis and treatment of a hyperactive animal are dramatic but no more vital than diagnosis and treatment of some very common health problems. The following table lists some physical ailments and related problem behaviors.

PHYSICAL PROBLEM	ASSOCIATED BEHAVIOR PROBLEMS
Urinary tract infection/inflammation Vaginal infection/inflammation	In-house urination; sexual mounting; self-mutilation; biting; chewing; false pregnancy; digging; barking; masturbation
Anal sac impaction—mild	House-soiling; aggressiveness; self-mutilation; overexcitability; barking; escaping; biting
Pancreatitis	Eating stools; poor learning; self-multilation; chewing; overeating; house-soiling
Visual problems: cataracts, optic nerve inflammation, brain-related causes and visual/motor complications.	Biting; fighting other dogs; aggressiveness; shyness; fear of objects, people, sounds; escaping; running away; chewing; poor learning leading to housetraining problems; self-mutilation
Hip dysplasia	Biting; shyness; self-mutilation; chewing; aggressiveness
Dental problems	Chewing; barking; biting; self-mutilation; digging; poor eating
Ear infections/deafness	Barking; biting; moodiness; chewing; lack of obedience; housetraining problems

While there are many other health problems that affect behavior, these conditions usually go undetected by owners.

It requires years of experience based on proper veterinary education to detect and treat ailments that affect behavior. Seemingly simple problems such as intestinal worms, a condition tolerated all too often by pet owners, can affect functions of the nervous system. The microscopic larvae of certain kinds of pervasive parasites can and do penetrate the brains of dogs and cats. Often there are behavioral changes before we even notice the physical effects of such illnesses. A simple stool sample and regular examination are a pets only protection against such ravages. However, the dog or cat cannot order it done; it is up to you and me.

Nutrition and Feeding

Your dog is a meat-eating predator by nature. If he were born in the wilderness in a pack of pet dogs gone wild, he would start eating the partially predigested contents of the stomachs of adult pack members as soon as he went off his mother's milk, between five and ten weeks of age. This food would be made up of parts of the animals killed and eaten by the grown-ups. The only vegetables involved would themselves have been predigested by prey. When old enough, he would start learning to kill and eat his own prey, which is a basic canine functional drive that domestication has made obsolete.

During the past fifty years or so, an entirely new nutritional industry has been developing—that of pet food. Before that time, pet

dogs ate pretty much what their ancient ancestors ate—leftovers from their human masters' meals. The pet food industry was founded as a means of utilizing (and selling) the waste by-products of the human food industry. For a long time the protein in dog food was largely useless to dogs; that is, it was crude protein, but little of it could be assimilated and utilized. Fortunately, thanks to pressure from numerous nutritional critics, the quality of commercial pet foods appear to be improving. There are now special diets for growth, adulthood, and old age, as well as for special physical conditions such as kidney, heart, and intestinal problems. Genetically based allergies have also generated specialized diets. So things are looking up for the nutritional needs of dogs. In the meantime, however, behavior problems can be created, made worse, or made easier to correct through enlightened nutritional treatment.

If your dog is hyper he may, for example, have a food allergy. Then again, he might need a different balance of dietary protein, carbohydrate, and fat. While some commercial dog foods advertise diets as "high protein" they are rarely more than 30 percent protein, while carbohydrates comprise more than 50 percent of the nutritional value. This is hardly high protein! Many dogs, as with humans, are carbohydrate sensitive and get hyper from too much grain starch and sugar. Increasing the protein in their diet, along with proper vitamin supplementation, actually calms them.

Many dogs that go through unreasonable mood swings from happy-go-lucky to aggressive are victims of allergies, often to certain foods that affect the function of the thyroid gland. The possible effects of diet on behavior seem limitless. At this time there are more mysteries than solutions. So what should the dog owner with a problem do?

The first step in diagnosing all behavior problems should be a health checkup. Veterinarians now have ways to test for and treat food allergies and hyperkinesis. When these tests prove positive, the treatment is usually convenient and economical. The hyper dog that calms down on a higher-protein or hypoallergenic diet merely needs to continue on that diet with a proper behavior program for a long, happy, well-behaved life.

If you find special diets too expensive, there are economical homebrew recipes available. Your veterinarian can either give them to you or advise where they can be obtained. Once the health of the problem dog has been addressed, the proper behavior program should be put into action and carried out for at least six weeks to ensure a permanent correction.

Nutrient Requirements

You have learned how nutrition can affect your dog's behavior. It is certainly true that dietary needs of a dog are the most misunderstood aspect of pet ownership, bar none. And no wonder. A few generations ago, dogs were fed leftovers from the family table and seemed to thrive. These usually included a little meat, some potatoes, greens, even bits of fresh salad—all the protein, carbohydrate, fat, fiber, minerals, and trace elements a dog needed to remain strong and healthy.

Then came modern food processing and the introduction of canned or otherwise preserved dog and cat foods. Some companies told us our dogs needed meat, while others claimed a balanced supply of protein, carbohydrates, fat, and other nutrients from vegetable sources would keep Fido in fine fettle.

The power of advertising has convinced the vast majority of dog owners that commercial pet foods are more convenient, more appealing, and more satisfying than table scraps, which is probably true.

Nutrition definitely affects behavior.

However, certain problems emerge from the conflict between a dog owner's desire to provide a stable, nutritious diet and the feeling that dogs also need variety to be happy.

This feeling about variety in taste appeal, color, and texture is strictly a projection of human eating habits. The fact of the matter is that dogs thrive on monotony in their diets. They retain better health, live longer, and are emotionally more stable eating the same complete, balanced commercial dog food every day of their lives.

On the other hand, if we occasionally make available some table tidbits, our pets can learn to love variety, too. This is where behavior problems can erupt; the dog may turn up his nose at commercial food or start to beg for people food, much to the dismay of the family at the dinner table, especially when there are guests.

Beggers and Finicky Eaters

If you are plagued by a finicky eater or a begging dog, follow this program and you should clear up the problem within about two weeks:

- Feed your dog his regular diet twice daily.

- If you do feed leftovers, place them in the dog's regular food dish at his regular feeding time and delete the amount of normal food equal to the amount of leftovers. If you can, stop feeding leftovers altogether. The dog will be better off for it.

- Before you sit down to eat, walk to a spot away from the table, but where the dog can see the table, and call the dog. When it arrives there, pet and praise it and tell it to stay. Even if you have to repeat this process many times during the meal, do it until your pet stays at that spot for the entire meal.

- When you have finished your meal, go over and praise the dog again away from the table. This will establish a happy ending for his self-control.

Follow this program until your dog simply goes naturally to his spot and remains there for the entire meal. Before two weeks have passed, even in the most stubborn cases, success should be achieved with this program.

Dietary Behavioral Problems

Obesity

Obesity in dogs can be attributed to one major cause: The pet is receiving too much of the wrong kind of food for his metabolic type and activity level. I have seen littermates proceed through life, one of them eating less than 60 percent of the same type of food as his brother, yet maintaining the same body weight. Each dog's system is unique. A little bit of starch may put weight on one animal, while another may burn rather than store the same starch.

If your pet is fat, consult with your veterinarian on a diet that will suit his individual metabolism, then stick to the diet for at least six weeks before you expect to see any dramatic changes in weight. Even if your dog seems wildly hungry, hold steady to the new diet. If it has been overfed in the past, several weeks must pass before his stomach shrinks to normal size. In the meantime it is normal for the dog to seem hungry all the time, since his stomach is still feeling unfilled, even though all the required nutrients are going into his system.

Keep in mind that fat dogs are the victims of our mismanagement of their diets. We hold their health and longevity in our hands. This means that any tidbitting must be stopped, in fairness to the pet. A dog of normal weight may outlive an obese pet by as much as 40 percent. A little human self-control can lead to many more years of delightful companionship with a healthy dog.

Food Stealing

Stealing food is as natural to dogs as any of their other more primitive behaviors. Historically, dogs are scavengers. Wild dogs specialize in teaming up to steal carcasses from other predators.

If you are unfortunate enough to have a food stealer, resign yourself to the fact that you will have to take careful precautions to control the problem. You have probably tried most of the traditional punishment and scolding routines, so it is best not to continue with these unsuccessful approaches.

There is one procedure that has worked well in many cases. It avoids physical punishment, but takes advantage of events that dogs may find unpleasant.

First, feed your dog twice a day. Then identify his "pet hate." Once discovered, this is used in association with food placed in spots where your dog may try to steal it. An example best illustrates the system.

A Norwegian Elkhound had the upsetting habit of raiding the hors d'oeuvre tray when the family had guests, the only occasions when food was on the coffee table. This dog's pet hate was getting his nails clipped. The owners were advised to keep the clippers handy. Each time the dog so much as looked toward the tray, they called it to them, near the tray, and pleasantly clipped a toenail. Before they had finished a pawful of nails, the dog actually went to a corner and remained there as if riveted whenever the Lazy Susan was produced!

Another case involved a giant German Shepherd that hated to be bathed. The same routine was followed, except each time food was left around, the bath water was turned on and the dog was called toward the food and then toward the bathroom. One week later, after five such sessions, the owners had the sweetest smelling, cleanest, non-food-stealing pet in the neighborhood.

Some other "treatments" have used ear and/or eye cleaning, putting on or taking off a collar, even going out on a cold night. Whatever your dog abhors, barring physical punishment, apply it to this system for at least two weeks for results that will be permanent. But remember, you still have to be careful about leaving morsels around when you are not there to oversee the situation.

I never advise putting the dog out of the area in isolation. This risks establishing an association between guests and being cut off from the family. Jealousy of guests, rather than avoidance of food, can result.

During any of the procedures involving food, remain good-natured, optimistic, and be patient with your dog. Behavior changes associated with food are the most difficult to achieve but are well worth the time and effort invested.

Analyzing and Treating the Cause of the Problem

Dogs don't often suffer, in the true sense of the word, from behavior problems; people do. In fact, as a general rule dogs rarely cause behavior problems. Owners are usually the culprits. Further, most so-called dog behavior problems don't even rate serious attention until they make people uncomfortable enough to do something about them. Then, all too often, the logical solution to the problem appears to be to "fix the dog." That is, when the dog is misbehaving, stop it and/or make it do something else. This is the *behavioristic approach*. It runs into difficulties because *it deals with symptoms*, such as the act of barking, *rather than causes*.

Another view considers anxiety to be the cause of the problem behavior. This method treats the anxiety. But it usually ignores the cause of the anxiety.

A third approach considers the total dog and his environment. It views the dog as more than a simple "behavioral model" responding to various stimuli by behaving in wanted or unwanted ways. This method recognizes a pet dog as a four-legged member of a two-legged family, with most of the emotional attachments and involvements of his human companions. It sees *unwanted behavior as a way for the dog to relieve the tension created by anxiety* which, in turn, is usually caused by frustration in the pet's life. For want of a more descriptive name, I'll call this a *causative approach* to behavior problems.

Deciding Which Approach to Use

To get a clear picture of how these three approaches work, let's analyze an actual case from my files. This is about a dog that barks when left alone. It represents a class of problems which poses the greatest challenge to behaviorists, since the misbehavior occurs when the owner is not at home to make corrections. To make it more interesting, we'll consider you are the dog's owner.

Your pet is a good-natured, medium-sized female, spayed terrier mix, two years old. She is in perfect health. You live alone in an adults-only apartment building and have had the same neighbors since your dog was a puppy. Until recently you and your neighbors all worked the usual five-day week, but then the man next door went on a midnight to 8:00 A.M. shift. You knew your dog barked when you went to work, but nobody complained, so it wasn't a problem. In fact, you felt lucky, because one neighbor had a dog that chewed up carpets when it was left alone. At least your Tippy's barking wasn't destructive. But last night your attitude changed. The landlord knocked on your door with a legal barking-dog complaint from the city's animal regulation department, plus an eviction warning.

Now who has a problem? Several parties, in fact! The neighbor who signed the complaint feels badly about it, but he has to sleep to keep working. The landlord, who dislikes evicting anyone, has to live by the rules, so he gives you the legal month to get the situation resolved, apologizes, and starts mentally preparing a want ad for your apartment. Do you have problems! All sorts of things go around in your head. You are ambivalent about the neighbor, whom you like, but you feel like calling him and saying, "Thanks, Ralph! At least you could've spoken to me about it before you called the law! And by the way, forget about that patio barbecue next Saturday night!" But you get a handle on your emotions and investigate ways to solve the problem and remain in your happy home.

What to do? You call your veterinarian, who recommends that you phone me. I give you a rundown on your alternatives in a framework of possible approaches to a correction and usual results.

There are variations on these approaches, but the theme remains the same—treat the barking behavior and/or the anxiety. Both of these approaches ignore an important fact: what goes on between owners and dogs when they are home together influences how the dogs behave when the owners are away. With this in mind, let's go deeper, applying the principles of pet dog behavior using an approach to your problem that reaches beyond simple barking behavior or anxiety, and looks at what is going on in your day-to-day life with the terrier.

The Causative Approach

What is causing the frustration that creates the anxiety and tension the dog is attempting to relieve by barking? When you uncover the answer to this question, and do something about it, the barking usually stops in an incredibly short time—a couple of days in some cases and as long as six weeks in others. However, there's a catch. *You are the only person who knows what's bugging your dog, and only you can take the steps necessary to correct the situation and make the threat of eviction go away.* So, we make an appointment for an interview at your apartment. At the appointed time, the doorbell rings.

For the moment we'll ignore exactly what is being said in our conversation and describe what physical behavior is occurring. As the doorbell rings, the dog runs to the door ahead of you. You open the door, trying to get your leg between Tippy and me. We exchange greetings while Tippy is jumping up and yipping at both. I reach to pet Tippy, who rolls onto her side. I pet her briefly. You close the door and gesture toward the living room. The dog runs ahead and jumps and yips at me while I sit. You sit on a chair opposite me and call Tippy to you. She ignores you. You stand and start toward us, calling the dog. Tippy rolls onto her side again. You pick her up, return to the chair, and put her down into a sitting position at your feet.

The conversation continues while Tippy whines. You say "No" to her, shaking her by the scruff of her neck. You get up to go to the kitchen to turn on the coffee maker. Tippy races after you. I get out my notepad and make notes. Tippy returns to the room, followed by you. You call Tippy to the chair, tell her to sit, and stroke her. She stays calm as long as you keep stroking, while the conversation continues. When you stop stroking, Tippy whines and gets restless. You stroke again. You get up to go to the kitchen for coffee and cups. There is the same routine, with Tippy following you out, leading you back. For the first half hour I ask questions, and you do most of the talking. Then, I explain my recommendations, writing on a form, showing it to you occasionally. I say you are about to learn the power of nonverbal communication with Tippy. Without speaking a word to the dog, you are about to teach her to stay by your chair while you go to the door to say good-bye to me, without any anxiety or excitement on the dog's part. You say, "Fat chance, Bill." We have a little chuckle and start the leadership routine, which goes as follows.

I start to stir, as if to get ready to leave, and you start to get up. Tippy starts wagging her tail and jumping again at me as I sidle toward the door. You go toward the door and Tippy runs ahead. Both you and I quickly return to our seats. Tippy leaves the door, tentatively, and returns to you, wagging her tail. You pet her briefly (two seconds).

You get up and start toward the door. Tippy rushes ahead; you instantly turn and go back to your seat. Tippy returns to you and you pet her briefly. You again get up and start to the door. Tippy sits at your chair, looking expectantly at you. You return to the chair and quietly praise and pet her briefly. This get up/go-to-door/return-pet routine goes on for fifteen minutes, until finally, you can open and close the door while Tippy remains at the chair.

I then accompany you to the door. Predictably, since she hasn't yet learned to stay away in this situation, Tippy leaves the chair and races ahead. We both quickly return to our chairs; so does Tippy. You pet her briefly. Only five minutes worth of the going/returning is required before Tippy remains at your chair while the door is opened for me to leave. You are able to say your good-byes in peace for the first time in your life in the dogs presence.

I leave you a sheet of instructions for your reference and a time for our next appointment. You return to your chair, a thoughtful expression on your face and the recommendation sheet in your hand. As you sit down, you absentmindedly reach down to start stroking Tippy, but suddenly you withdraw your hand. You smile, realizing you have just modified your own behavior and gained important insights about yourself and Tippy.

Let's peek at my private notepad to see what I wrote when you went to get the coffee. My first notes:

> 1. Tippy excitable, vocal, good-natured, bossy.
>
> 2. Tippy feels leader. Too dependent.
>
> 3. Physically dominant-negative vocal.
>
> 4. Fondling, too-long petting.

If we review the scenario, it becomes clearer where I got my diagnosis during the first part of the interview. Tippy's center-of-attention behavior during the greeting, her yips, and jumping resulted in note number 1. Tippy's leading into the living room, out of the kitchen, back to the door, and following you to the kitchen formed observation number 2.

Tippy's extremely submissive response to my reaching to pet, your own approach when she did not leave my chair, your loud "No" and scruff-shaking created comment number 3. Your continual stroking to keep Tippy calm accounted for number 4.

Now, on to outline what was said.

In the early part of the interview you told me about your workday and weekend routines. I also wanted to know about early house-training and behavior problems, especially how you handled them. You gave me good descriptions of your actions and Tippy's reactions. Here is a list of important practices and events, with recommended changes:

Event: You feed Tippy once a day, usually right after coming home in the early evening. This leaves Tippy with an empty stomach most of the day because food stays in her stomach only six to nine hours. Also, cramming a whole day's nutrient bulk into her tummy stretches it. Then, when it empties, it is a gaping emptiness. This creates restlessness in all animals. All Tippy's senses are "hyped." Like a once-a-day-fed zoo lion, she becomes anxious about her next meal.

I recommend: Split food in two; feed morning and evening, with the evening meal at least thirty minutes after the latest homecoming time in your schedule. This avoids the anxiety and "hunger tension" during the day.

Event: You jog with Tippy on weekend mornings but never during the week.

I recommend: Jog with her daily or leave her at home on weekend jogs. Either way provides the consistency Tippy needs.

Event: Before leaving for work, you pick up and cuddle Tippy, reassuring her you'll be back. You then put her down, away from the door, saying "Stay!" Then you hurry out as Tippy rushes to the closing door. This ritual of guilt helps to impress Tippy, emotionally, that "something really is wrong." She cannot understand exactly what is wrong, but she feels anxious and frustrated.

I recommend: Sit quietly for at least five minutes before you leave her. Use the walk-to-door, then return routine, without speaking, in place of "Stay," until Tippy stays away from the door. Then leave, without speaking.

Event: At homecoming you and Tippy have a joyous greeting ritual at the door.

I recommend: This builds too much apprehension during the day for Tippy's excitable nervous system to tolerate. Instead, walk in, say "Hi, Tippy," avoid eye contact, then do your other activities for at least five minutes. You may then greet Tippy, away from the front door area.

Event: Whenever Tippy nudges you for affection, you stroke her until she leaves or stops nudging. This "Tippy nudges/you respond" routine makes her feel she is the leader in your relationship. Also, whenever you get the urge to give her affection, you go to her to pet and cuddle her.

I recommend: She is never expected to do anything to earn praise and petting. Prolonged stroking creates an overdependence on your presence. When you leave, she feels overstressed without her petting machine. Do not withhold affection or petting, but ask her to learn to earn praise and petting. In other words, satisfy some of her need to function for a leader.

This routine has been nicknamed the "no free lunch program." It goes like this: Ask Tippy to come or sit when you get the urge to give affection or she asks for it. Then pet her, briefly (less than five seconds), and avoid prolonged stroking. Speak your commands softly, pleasantly.

Event: You taught Tippy to "speak" for food treats but rarely do it except when company is present.

I recommend: Do not tidbit Tippy. It has become tied to barking and can compound your problem. Besides, she is performing for the food, rather than for you.

You follow my advice, but it is tough on you. After all, the very reason you got Tippy was to enjoy those homecomings and all that stroking. It is kind of flattering to have a pet who shows that she doesn't want you to leave her. However, after a few days of your leadership by movement and no-free-lunch procedures, Tippy seems so much calmer and less frustrated; you persevere.

Improvement is seen during the first week and all unreasonable barking is gone by the middle of the second week. Two further complaints by the neighbor were due to Tippy's barking when salespeople rang your doorbell, which the law allows. You followed my advice and got a "Day sleeper: Do Not Disturb" sign for your door.

By the way, you did get together with your formerly unhappy neighbor for that barbecue. And Tippy didn't even beg for tidbits!

Techniques to Avoid

Techniques I **do not** consider appropriate in solving dog behavior problems are:

Electrical Shock Devices

Even with fancy labels such as "hi-tech" and "electrical stimulation," shocking a pet dog to control unwanted behavior is a quick-fix method that is totally out of step with enlightened, humane approaches. It can also lead to aggression, displacement behavior problems, and ustable behavior.

Cages

I have never found caging necessary. I also never recommend putting a dog outdoors, in garages, bedrooms, or closets as a means of "psychological" punishment for misbehavior.

Rough Handling

Shaking, hitting, or roughly pressing a dog into submission are not necessary to gain leadership. This type of correction has the possibility of causing unwanted side effects, such as submissive wetting or biting. It can even injury a puppy's nervous system.

Other physical measures that I do *not* recommend are "kneeing" your dog in the chest, stepping on his toes, throwing the dog on his back to stop jumping, or submerging the dog's head in a water-filled, freshly dug hole, until the animal goes limp to correct digging.

These heavy-handed measures are more likely to damage your relationship with your pet than solve problem behavior.

Food Rewards

Food rewards are potent motivators, but fail to address the *causes* of unwanted behavior. Remember Tippy's case!

CORRECTING BEHAVIOR PROBLEMS

INTRODUCTION TO SECTION III

RMM's engaging cartoons are the only thing that will keep you from falling asleep in fifteen minutes if you try to read this section as if it were a "book." There is a lot of repetition because the basis for correcting so many problems involves some of the same basic procedures. However, I did not want to leave out any of the elements, because you will be referring to the individual program as you go through it with your pet.

Read the correction program for your problem as if you were going to have to take an oral examination on it. That way you will commit it to memory and put every element to work. Each correction program has been used successfully by hundreds of thousands of dog owners, who have received pamphlet versions of these programs through their veterinarians (*BehavioR$_x$ Series,* by William Campbell). With patience and optimism, you can have a pet that adds joy to your life.

Aggression Toward Owners

This program deals with outright biting and emerging aggression shown by growling. Though the text uses the term "biting," you can substitute the word "growl" if your pet has not yet bitten, but appears on the verge of it.

The reasons for bites or growls may involve anything from overprotectiveness of food, toys, and other articles, to a response to scolding or punishment. Simply adapt the principles to your situation, since the same correction routine applies to all these problems.

When your own dog helps itself to some of your flesh, this is the ultimate insult. If ever I have heard a classic description of "ambivalence," it comes from bite victims. "I wanted to kill that so-and-so, but I was shocked and my feelings were hurt to the quick," is the usual kind of statement. Also, most people say they aren't sure they can trust or feel the same warmth and affection for their pet ever again. The meaning of the statement "Once bitten, twice shy" becomes painfully clear. It is extremely difficult to behave toward the dog with the same confidence as before. The dog senses this change and may take advantage of it, depending on the circumstances that led to the bite.

To start rehabilitating your relationship in a way that will also rebuild your confidence and allow you to correct the problem, you'll have to analyze what type of biting occurred.

Reasonable versus Unreasonable Biting

All biting can probably be classified as defensive, in that it results from the dog feeling threatened. For instance, if you were bitten while applying some physical punishment, it's simple to deduce that the biting was defensive. On the other hand, if you were merely telling the dog to get off the couch, using no threatening gestures, it is hard to say that the bite was defensive. However, in the couch situation, it was the dog's "status" (its feeling of dominance over you) that was threatened. In either case, the basic program for correction follows the same course.

"Can you give him something to relax his jaws?"

It is not unreasonable for a dog that feels he is the "boss" of his people to growl at, or even bite, his underlings if human underlings want to pet the boss dog. Extremely bossy dogs tell their people when and for how long they are permitted to pet them, not vice versa. Therefore, even though it may seem unreasonable, touching such a dog, even affectionately, when he is not in the mood, threatens his dominant status.

This kind of dog, basically a leader, dominant and/or independent type, can be classified as "spoiled rotten." We'll call his biting "reasonable," at least to the dog!

The genuinely "unreasonable" biter seems to suffer episodes of insanity. It might be better to say that people suffer from his brief episodes, since some of these dogs, after biting with apparently vicious intent, wag their tails, act submissively, and literally lick the wounds they inflicted a few moments before.

These pets require a great deal more medical attention than their owners usually afford them. They should be given complete physical and neurologic examinations. If the dog is a purebred, the breeder should make a contribution to the cost, especially for a genetic chromosomal analysis. I find that many unreasonable biters suffer from arthritis, hip dysplasia, thyroid dysfunction (usually low), hormone imbalances, hydrocephalus (too much brain fluid pressure), cataracts, prediabetic and diabetic conditions, or even foxtails (grass awns) in the ears. If it is your fate to have such a dog, I hope you will consider medical examination as a reasonable approach to unreasonable behavior.

If your dog bites an infant or child under the age of about six but has not shown aggression to adults or other family children, your best bet is to follow the programs for Biting (chapter 14) and for Babies, New Pets, and Dogs (chapter 12) which apply to such situations. This program is for family members old enough to understand its content and/or carry it out with parental supervision every step of the way.

Don't Punish

Physical punishment must be avoided if this program is to be effective. If your biter bit in reaction to physical punishment, this should seem obvious. On the other hand, if the dog was punished after some biting incident and biting is still a problem, the message must be the same: Do not use it.

The same holds true for "psychological" punishment, such as putting the dog outside. If this practice has not succeeded to date, it probably never will.

The program also assumes you have tried the "shame on you" and "bad dog" routines with no improvement in the behavior problem. So scolding must also be avoided.

The Hyperkinetic Biter

Hyperkinetic dogs, like their child counterparts, are constantly on the move, always seeking attention. They are four-legged response mechanisms looking for a stimulus. I have even seen them bump into chairs, just to get the feedback of the chair's movement! When hyperkinetics also bite, they are usually deemed "psychotic" because their total behavior seems unreasonable.

Physically they may appear normal, but most of those I have met have slightly enlarged pupils, even on bright, sunny days. Compared to normal dogs, they drink very little water. When held in mild restraint their heart and breathing rates go sky high. Some of them salivate a great deal, but they usually swallow their saliva.

It is important not to confuse a hyperexcitable dog with a genuine hyperkinetic. Hyperexcitable dogs overreact to activities around them. Hyperkinetics do not need activities around them; they are always on the move, making things happen around them.

Many hyperkinetics respond well to a medication that would make a normal dog (or child) hyperactive. Instead, genuine hyperkinetics calm down dramatically and appear to become normal. Often the hyperkinetic biter ceases to show any hostile behavior. If this occurs, the dog can be worked through a program of biting correction and will respond even more quickly than the nonhyperkinetic biter.

Both the medical and behavioral programs for correction in these cases need veterinary supervision and guidance. However, they are well worth the time and effort required.

Corrective Program

Social Distance

To change your relationship with your biting dog, you must put some "social distance" between you and him. This does not mean physical distance. Rather, it means that interactions between you and your dog should be unemotional. To accomplish this, all you need to do is take care of the dog's physical needs. This should involve the following, and no more:

- Feed it on a twice-a-day schedule.

- Keep its water bowl full.

- Let it outside or take it out for toilet duties only. If you have been taking it for walks, suspend them until later in the program.

- Avoid all eye contact with the dog.

- Do not speak to the dog, except when absolutely necessary.

- Avoid physical contact with it, except as required for its well-being. For instance, if the dog comes over and leans on you, or gets onto the furniture, merely move away in a neutral manner.

These steps avoid emotional interchange between you and the dog, and set the stage for a revised relationship. This shows itself in many ways. The dog may increasingly try to get your attention, or he may even "pout" for a couple of days. If he tries the pouting routine, let him, and wait until it starts soliciting your attention for petting or praise.

This cooling-off period allows you to assess your own feelings about both the biting incident and the dog. When you feel the dog is trying to warm up to you, and when you feel confident in renewing your emotional and physical relationship (petting, not punishing), the time is usually right to start reestablishing a proper social standing with your pet—one in which you are the leader. This usually takes two to four days.

Determining the Subproblem and Earning Leadership

Getting bitten by your own dog usually happens because of some other behavior problem. If this is the case, consult the appropriate problem program (Chewing, chapter 17; Jumping, chapter 24; Barking, chapter 13; etc.) and follow that program *in conjunction with this one.*

If your pet is to recognize you as his leader, you must function as a leader. Tell the dog to do something, such as "Tippy, Sit," each time he asks for your attention and/or petting. If the dog is already sitting, tell him to lie down. Briefly praise and pet happily for obedience. Do not ask him to sit for dinner or breakfast or tidbits of food. You want the dog functioning for you, not for food. Besides, "the hand that feeds" has already been bitten!

If you were bitten in a situation such as when telling the dog to get off the furniture or while handling the dog, you need to understand that the dog bit to put you in "underling" status.

When You've Got "IT"

"IT" is having control over your dog's feelings, as well as his behavior. You can tell by the dog's reactions to your praise, after he responds to the command sit or down.

You won't have "IT" if, instead of sitting, the dog starts jumping on you or moves away, or if he barks or pouts, which may happen with extremely bossy dogs.

You will have "IT" when you see your pet's emotional energy and attention directed to what you want, rather than what he wants. When you feel you have this control, you can start the correction program for the other behavior problem, if there was one that led to the biting in the first place.

Applying the Jolly Routine

What I refer to as the "Jolly Routine" is simply a method of conditioning your dog with distraction. You must recreate, or be vigilant to take advantage of the problem situation should it be one that is difficult to arrange such as coming home and finding the dog on the furniture.

The instant the dog notices you and is in the situation, clap your hands and say anything that will cause the dog to wag his tail. You know what phrases "turn on" your dog, so use them. Some examples are:

"Good dog, Tippy. Let's get the ball!"

"Good dog, Tippy. Wanna go out?"

As you say the good-time phrase, move away from the dog and toward the ball, the door, and so forth. Get the dog to follow you. Do not approach the dog. If he follows, play with the ball or follow through on the activity that started the routine.

If the dog bit in a semidark situation, follow the jolly phrase by turning on adequate light as you move away and attract the dog out of the situation.

If possible, go through the Jolly Routine a couple of times a day, but do not repeat it more than twice in a single situation. Its impact can be diluted if overdone. Besides, the new emotional reactions need time to incubate for the dog to be able to retain them.

If you follow the principles involved in the cooling-off period, and apply the leadership and jolly phases with confidence, you should be back on an even keel with your dog after six weeks. In the event you do not seem to be getting anywhere with this program, you could benefit from the services of an experienced dog behavior consultant.

REMEMBER:
Never create a situation or go into a session unless you feel you have control over the dog's mood. If you feel shaky, your heart is in your mouth, or your pulse is pounding, return to the "Earning Leadership" phase until you have settled down and feel confident again. Always keep in mind that with an extremely bossy dog you must make leadership the hallmark of your lifelong relationship.

Babies, New Pets, and Dogs

The introduction of a new baby or animal into the household of an established dog requires some thoughtful preparation. If the established pet is normal, healthy, and well-adjusted, the joy of the occasion should be reflected in his behavior-good-natured curiosity about the newcomer. There are, however, several steps that ought to be taken to ensure an emotionally upbeat tone to the proceedings.

Preparing the Pet

Analyze the relationships between everyone in the household and the pet. Are they positive? Are the people in the family praising and petting for good behavior? What negative aspects are there in the relationships? If there is more negative than positive, then turn this around and work on the problems. An example will help explain this.

A young couple expecting a baby had a small terrier which they had allowed on the furniture when he was a puppy, but then decided to keep off the sofa and chairs. Though they had tried all sorts of measures, including punishment, the dog would jump onto the sofa when the owners were away. This brought about a situation where the dog was scolded almost daily when the owners arrived home to find it just getting off the furniture, or found telltale dog hair thereon. However, both husband and wife admitted they sometimes weakened and allowed the dog up with them, but only on special occasions in the evenings. Otherwise the relationships were excellent among them. With the coming of the new baby, though, they decided this practice should be stopped for hygienic reasons. They felt the dog might have fleas or be a carrier of some disease that could be transmitted to the child.

When the newborn baby was brought home, the terrier, quite normally, was extremely curious about it, wanting to jump up, sniff, and investigate. The parents scolded the dog and put him out of the house. The result was that the dog, a male, started urinating in the house, especially in the baby's room if the door was left open. The problem

became worse when the dog was punished after the urine marks were found. Within a couple of weeks the usually happy dog started skulking whenever the baby was present and would not come near it. The owners became worried enough to seek professional advice.

The situation in this case appeared obvious when viewed from outside: Jealousy resulted from an association by the dog between the arrival of the baby and the disapproval, even rejection, by his cherished owners. The solution also seemed obvious but required a change in the attitudes of the owners. The baby's pediatrician agreed that if the parents were worried about fleas and disease, the answer was to keep both dog and household flea-free. A trip to the veterinarian ensured the proper procedure was followed to get rid of any fleas and assured the parents of the animal's excellent health. This included a regular schedule of bathing for the terrier.

Besides these measures, the owners followed a program of praising the pet each time they brought the baby around or paid attention to it. They taught the dog to sit by the sofa, and held the child so the terrier could smell it—all done with happy, praising words for the situation. The result was that the pet soon wagged his tail whenever the baby got attention, since it now was a shared, totally positive attention. The urination problem disappeared overnight.

This case highlights one of the major concerns about newcomers, whether babies, animals, or guests. The best procedure is to make the arrival a happy one that includes the established pet. Better yet, the arrival should mean the animal gets more, rather than less, attention than before. This is when a most important steps to prepare the pet are necessary.

How Much Attention?

Your pet is highly sensitive to the amount and nature of attention you give him. In preparing for the newcomer, take stock of how much, and at what times you are giving attention to the established pet. For instance, if you feed him at 8:00 A.M. and 6:00 P.M. and the schedule will have to be delayed when the newcomer arrives, adjust the feeding time at least four days before that occasion. This avoids any association between the arrival and the delayed feedings.

If you feel you pay constant attention to your pet, especially if he demands it, cut down on the amount of attention a couple of weeks before the new arrival. However, do not cut down on the positive quality of the attention you give the animal. If anything, intensify it; make him more happy.

If you spend a good deal of time absentmindedly petting your dog or cat, remember that the animal will sorely miss this if he cannot continue when the newcomer appears. Jealousy could result, and problems crop up.

One of the best ways to prepare a pet that constantly demands petting is to teach him to do something for the petting, such as sit. This is a fairly simple exercise that most dogs already know how to perform and it can be used anytime. **The plan is simply to ask for a sit each time the animal seeks petting. Rather than prolonged stroking, make it a brisk, upbeat, brief petting. Then, go on with some other activity.** This will be especially necessary after a new baby arrives. Preparing the pet for it in this way avoids the possibility of the established animal's association between newcomer and any deprivation.

Personal Contact

How closely should a pet and new baby be allowed contact? This should be discussed with the pediatrician. The doctor knows your child, his state of health, and immunization schedule. On the other hand, your veterinarian knows the state of your pet's health. A thorough examination a few days before the arrival should be scheduled. At that time any possible problems can be discussed with your pet's doctor. Thereafter, it is a matter of personal preference. Many parents are comfortable allowing their pets to enjoy extremely close contact with their babies, even sniffing and licking them. Others are more reserved. The plan that works best is one which ensures that the pet does not see the newcomer as an interloper. Rather, the interpretation should be that the newcomer means more positive attention than before the arrival. This avoids jealousy and problems.

Use Your Judgment

You are more sensitive to your pet than any outsider who offers advice. If you feel uncomfortable about introducing a new baby or another pet into the household, so will your pet. This is because your dog probably has more emotional empathy (feels as you feel) with you than with any other being in his life. Therefore, if you feel that the dog is not safe around babies, do not expose the baby to situations which might be dangerous. However, avoid making your pet feel left out. For instance, if yours is an outside dog, intensify your contact with him outside. Do not let the dog feel abandoned after the newcomer arrives. Instead, make him feel he is getting more and better attention.

When Babies Crawl and Walk

Maturing babies not only look different when they start to move about, they also undergo changes in body chemistry and smell different, especially to animals. The first time your baby starts crawling, the dog might be quite surprised. He may want to investigate the baby more closely, might show casual interest, or even be startled and act upset about it. At this time it is up to you to show the pet how to interpret the baby's new-found mobility. Appear happy about the situation, and chances are the dog will feel likewise.

When the baby starts to crawl or walk toward the dog, follow the Jolly Routine. If the dog appears edgy about the baby's approach, happily praise him. Avoid scolding and do not grab the baby away. This can make the dog feel that the baby needs punishing or that something is genuinely wrong with the situation.

Just as dogs like to investigate babies, there comes a time when babies want to investigate dogs. It is not wise to leave babies and dogs in an unsupervised situation where the baby might inadvertently hurt or corner the animal. Unfortunately, babies usually want to poke their fingers into the dog's ears and eyes, which is understandably upsetting to the pet.

Babies do not walk; they toddle. A dog cornered by an approaching toddler, may feel threatened and defend itself by escaping, growling (which the baby does not understand), or snapping. Therefore, it is good practice to supervise the early interactions between nearly mobile babies and your dog. Show your pet a happy interpretation for the baby's activities, and a better lifelong relationship will result.

Barking

If your dog is a problem barker the odds are pretty good that it either bothers you directly, or complaining neighbors bother you indirectly. If it is the neighbors, then the barking probably occurs while you are away from home.

Why would a dog bark constantly? Our experience indicates that *most dogs bark either at some person, animal, or object, or about some condition such as being left alone, isolated from people or other dogs.*

It is normal for dogs to bark at animals and people entering the property or passing by. Some cities even define this logically as "reasonable" barking. However, when barking becomes a problem it is necessary to understand why and how it started if we are to correct it effectively and humanely.

Corrective Program

To correct the problem, a twofold program must be applied: The barking must be curtailed directly, and its cause must be dealt with. I have seen countless barking problems cleared up in a trice, simply by changing a yard-dog's situation. The dog was left inside the house!

Most people with yard-barkers say the dog is not house trained or chews if left inside. If this is your case it would be easier to deal with house training or chewing than the barking problem. Also, if your outdoor dog has matured since displaying the house problem, you might try leaving it inside for short periods for a few days. Then lengthen the time over about a week's span. You may find the old problem has cleared up by itself through maturity, and your barking problem is corrected as well.

Excessive Barking

The cause for much excessive barking often stems from early, unconscious training by dog owners themselves. That is, when the puppy first shows signs of territorial defense the owners are delighted and may even urge the pet to carry on.

The best way to handle it **when a pup first starts barking** is to call him to you and then go to investigate the situation quietly. This shows the pup through your behavior how you would like him to behave. Of course, if something is really amiss, the pup will start barking again and the result is a dependable watchdog.

Unfortunately, many people bark back at their problem barkers, by shouting. Since this rarely works except when you are at home, all the dog learns is that you are boss-barker. When you are gone, the dog becomes boss and continues.

When your dog starts to bark in your presence, call him to you as quietly as the barking will allow. If the barking was about something you feel needs attention, go investigate, but do so quietly. "Shush" the dog if he starts to bark again. After this procedure, go back and settle down, calling the pet to you to keep him close by.

Be persistent with this routine for up to six weeks. Soon you will see the dog look to you after his first bark, and that is good watchdog behavior.

When You're Away

Correction of barking when you are not at home is more complicated. **Territorial barking** is natural to dogs, a part of their functional makeup. However, the dog that makes a full-time job of it, even when everyday happenings take place, needs some other "function" to replace territoriality.

First it will be necessary to get the dog responding to you. The most effective device for this is your pet's need for approval. Therefore, whenever he approaches you for petting and attention you must ask him to do something, such as sit, before petting and praising him. Everyone in the household must follow this plan. It will teach the dog that he must do something (function) to earn petting, praise, and approval.

All fondling (prolonged petting) must be stopped or the program cannot succeed. It is a sacrifice, but the barking problem too often relates to a bossy, spoiled dog. And fondling spoils many dogs, especially barkers.

When you have used the sit-for-petting routine for about two days you are ready to make a setup to correct the barking that occurs when you are not at home.

Sneak'n Peek

A little detective work is now called for. When does your pet bark? Is it right after you leave home? If so, you will have to leave earlier than usual and apply the corrections to be detailed later.

Does the barking occur just before, or at the moment you arrive home? Then you will need to make arrangements to get home a few minutes earlier than normal for a few days. In either of the two situations you may need help from someone else if you cannot vary your schedule. Just be sure the person helping you understands the program.

I call this correction "sneak'n peek." It is applied earlier than your usual time for leaving or arriving home and also on the days you do not work. Make all your usual arrangements for leaving and then sit down quietly for at least five minutes in the area where you leave your dog. Pay no attention to the dog. Get up and leave without a word, start the car and drive away; do whatever makes the dog think you are truly gone.

Then sneak back to an area adjacent to the dog, but out of his sight and scenting ability (downwind, if outside). The instant the dog displays any sign that he may start barking, or if he does start, apply a "distraction." The distraction must be some sound other than your voice, and it must be quick, less than a second in duration, to be successful. One rap on a window, door, or fence usually succeeds in interrupting the dog's attention from the barking but avoids discovery of just where the distraction came from. If possible, make your observa-

Problem = Barking Dog

Solution	Usual outcome

When dog starts to bark, teach it to lie down; dogs can't bark while lying down.

Not so. Dog either learns to bark while prone, or waits until you're gone to bark.

Shout at dog to stop barking; scold or punish.

Dog stops barking when you shout, scold or punish. Waits until you've gone to start again.

Problem = Barking Dog
(continued)

Solution   **Usual Outcome**

Muzzle the dog.   Muffled barking, thirsty dog.

Strap on an electric shock col-   May stop barking when collar is
lar; "zap" dog when it barks.   on, but heightens anxiety and
                                   dog may substitute other be-
                                   havior, such as chewing furni-
                                   ture, self.

Surgically remove dog's vocal   Dog screams, may start barking
cords.   again if cords grow back.

Problem = Barking Dog
(continued)

Treat anxiety by getting dog to sit quietly before you leave it, instead of acting anxious, excitable. Give it a delicious tidbit as reward.

Fat, barking dog.

Treat anxiety by giving dog tranquilizer, sleeping pill, or other medication.

Calm, or sleepy, barking dog, Sometimes stops barking, but drugs have long-term adverse side-effects. Barking recurs when drug withdrawn.

tion point behind the dog when his attention is toward his usual barking target.

When the barking stops, do not praise the dog. Remain silent and repeat the distraction if the barking starts again or if you see or hear the dog getting ready to bark. Keep up this routine until your dog settles down.This may take from a few minutes to an hour, but it must be done. If you have to go to work before success is achieved, do not worry. It will take a little longer but will eventually produce results.

You will know you are making headway when you notice the dog perk up to a sound that used to cause barking, but settle down or merely whine or sniff in the direction of the sound.

If this entire program is applied for six weeks, you should be the owner of a dependable watchdog that does not bark at unimportant sounds and events, but will sound the alarm when something poses a genuine threat to you or your property. The sneak'n peek portion of the program may require only one or two sessions to succeed, but the entire sit-for-petting routine must be adhered to for six weeks.

> **Be consistent and patient with your dog. The reward will outweigh the sacrifices you make in what is a vexing problem for all concerned: you, the neighbors, and the dog as well.**

Biting

Everyone recognizes biting as a serious problem and wants it corrected immediately. However, a totally successful program requires six weeks or more.

Why Dogs Bite

The real solution lies first in understanding why your dog bit someone. Was he frightened? If so, what was he frightened of and for how long? Did he feel threatened? What was being threatened: his "people," his territory, his physical well-being, his self-esteem? When you have answered these questions you are starting on the road to a correction.

If your dog bites due to genuine fear of harm to himself, and if he otherwise is a happy, tail-wagging pet when you display happiness yourself, then a properly conducted program should correct the problem in about six weeks.

On the other hand, if your pet is a stoic and never wags his tail to show he is happy, then correction takes more time and care.

Correction of any type of biting entails more than merely doing things to the pet. It is also important to change things around the dog, perhaps even your own attitude or that of others.

First, everyone must sit down and discuss the first time the dog displayed either fearful or assertive, bossy behavior. How did you react to these early situations?

If the dog was fearful, did you try to reassure him with a sympathetic tone, even petting it? If so, your actions actually communicated to the dog that there really was something to be worried about. In other words, you did the wrong thing.

On the other hand, if you scolded or punished the dog, you also made a mistake. This is because the dog very often associates the feeling of rejection from such treatment with the people to whom he

showed fear or aggression. Thereafter the dog may become fearful or even vicious when these or other people visit or approach him.

Another cause of dog bites is often the very people who get bitten. A question I always ask is,"How many times has the victim been bitten and by how many dogs?" A goodly number of cases indicate that some folks are just prone to getting bitten. Unwittingly they show fear or hostility, either of which upsets some dogs.

One way they do it is by standing stock still. Absolute stillness, especially on first meetings, is a prelude to attack in the canine kingdom. Another victim "keeps an eye" on the dog. The result is another threat. Staring challenges the dog to be aggressive.

Others may approach dogs too frontally, too quickly, or even grab them by the necks or heads to get a "kiss." Children, especially, often scream hysterically around dogs, which can trigger the dog to chase and bite. Some victims blow in the animal's ear or otherwise tease him.

Unless teasing by the victim is involved, your biting dog must be shown how to enjoy these situations, and the victims must learn new behavior around your dog.

In the case of the teasers I recommend that you explain the situation to them and, if they do not change their behavior, put away your dog at least thirty minutes before they visit your home. Better yet, don't even invite these people to visit.

Some dogs with hair that hangs over their eyes tend to become biters. If you have such a dog, do your pet a favor and tie the hair up or better yet, cut it off. This will avoid visual surprises when people reach to pet or pick up the dog. Contrary to a popular myth, "hairy-eyed" dogs do not go blind when their eyes are exposed to sunlight.

Corrective Program

Defense Reflexes

Before detailing your program we need to discuss different types of defense reflexes in dogs. *A dog reacts in one of three ways to a threat: toward it, away from it, or freezes. Fight, flight, or freeze.* These behaviors occur only in the face of what the dog feels to be extreme threats.

Many dogs seem to belie their basic defensive behavior by acting otherwise at other times. For instance, I often see dogs that are quite vicious to nonfamily members, but show submissive behavior to the family, even when severely punished. I have also seen the opposite situation; the dog bites only family members and shows submissiveness to outsiders!

All this happens because of the way the dog "feels" about the situations. Feelings and emotions, not intelligence, probably dominate 99 percent of the interactions between us and our dogs.

Since it is emotional reactions that trigger biting, then all the "training" in the world (getting the dog to respond to some command) does not reach the heart of the problem.

Though you and all those around the dog will have to get your dog to sit before being praised or petted, this serves only to make the dog function for his praise. In other words, it orients your dog toward your position as leader.

The Jolly Routine

The key to gaining new emotional reactions to formerly threatening circumstances lies in the Jolly Routine. It requires you taking your dog into the situations that make him feel threatened. At that instant you must clap your hands once, then introduce an activity that causes happy feelings. This may be bouncing a ball, acting happy yourself, speaking a phrase, jingling car keys, or any such device, so as to switch the dog's emotional response from fear or hostility to jollity.

This must be repeated until the dog shows the happy behavior without having to use the Jolly Routine.

You may find the trigger stimulus for your dog's aggression or fear is the doorbell, footsteps on the walk, or the sight of a child or adult. Whatever it is, when you gain a jolly reaction to the first trigger, you may take the dog further into the situation, by careful steps, until you achieve the "jollies" from the beginning to the end of such situations. Then go on to different people and situations until you both feel comfortable in all situations.

> **Warning:** If you do not feel confident doing this routine with your dog off his leash, but feel comfortable with the leash, then use the leash. Do not risk communicating your tensions to the dog. It can make things worse, not better.

Body Language

When you have the ability to use the leash, make sure you are standing beside the dog's head or beside the person who is helping you. If you cannot do this, find a competent, humane trainer who will teach you to do so. Do not carry out this program until you feel competent. Did you notice I said standing beside the person helping? When a dog sees you beside a person he perceives you as on that individual's side, in favor of that person. Body positions speak like thunder to dogs.

When you face a person the dog sees you in a position of physical confrontation. The same body language holds true between the dog and others. Many dogs relax when a person simply turns sideways to them. This position signals friendliness. Many a dog takes reassurance if people crouch down, especially with one side to the dog.

Analyze your dog's reactions to all of these aspects, then integrate them into your program for correction. Now you have the ingredients:

- All the family members discuss the history to discover the original causes for the problem.

- Pet the dog only when he has sat for you.

- Avoid fondling. (Fondling makes biting dogs feel selfish about their relationships with people and inclined to object to anyone interrupting this selfish relationship.)

- Find the key to the Jolly Routine for your pet and apply it the instant the trigger stimulus occurs.

- Carefully go step by step through the biting situations until rehabilitation is complete.

- If your dog never wags his tail or acts happy, before starting this program you must create some key to the Jolly Routine and then start the program.

- Apply the Jolly Routine daily if you can; otherwise do it as often as possible, but success will take a little longer.

Puppy Problems

Finally, let us talk about puppies and their tendencies to bite or be mouthy with people. First, avoid tug-of-war with such pups. Do not tease them to the point that they snarl. Such treatment only teaches the pup to use his jaws and teeth with people.

As a correction for the nippy pup, pinch one of his rear feet when he starts to nip or mouth; this works marvelously if applied properly. Dogs have a defensive reflex basic to survival when some unexpected, possibly harmful, thing contacts their feet. The reflex is to withdraw. On the other hand, the basic biting reflex is hooked up to the body, neck, and head, particularly the snout. Therefore nipping or pinching these areas stimulates more biting!

The secret with puppies as well as older dogs is consistency. Be patient as you deal with your pet and do not expect overnight success. Biting can be solved by informed, consistent treatment.

A postscript: If you have considered that neutering your pet may help your program, discuss this with your veterinarian and follow his or her advice strictly.

Car Sickness

To appreciate fully the problem of car sickness we have to project to the dog some human sensations. Dogs suffer motion sickness in the same situations as people do, and they respond well to medical and behavioral therapy. This program for car sickness has helped thousands of dog owners who have followed it. It can help you and your pet as well.

Know the Cause

There are several causes for car sickness. One is created when a new puppy, already upset about being taken from his litter, is further upset by the car ride to his new home. If the puppy tends toward motion sickness, he will probably start salivating and then vomit. If the new owners then make too big a fuss over the puppy, pour on too much sympathy, or otherwise get upset, he senses that something is genuinely wrong, and the seeds are thus sown for future car sickness.

The way puppy owners react to situations provides a model for the way the pup will react. I call this the interpretive factor, and it is usually more important than the fact that the puppy got sick in the first place. It is far better to ignore the car sickness than to overreact emotionally, no matter how sympathetic we may feel.

Puppies that have been handled very little often suffer from car sickness. In dogs and people there is an area of the brain called the vestibular center that integrates many of the sensory impressions we receive. It is especially important in the condition of visual, tactile (touch), and balance functions. In very young animals this brain center needs to be stimulated if proper sensory integration is to develop.

Dogs that get carsick often lack this early handling and stimulation. There has been little experience of getting picked up, turned about, and cuddled upside down. Later, these dogs may tend to be car sickness victims. This is not to suggest that if you have a carsick six-month-old big dog you should start hoisting him up as part of your correction program. But if you have a pup or small breed it might be helpful if you do it gently a couple of times a day.

Visual causes are also akin to human experience. Many children who are forced to sit in the back seat get carsick. So do many dogs. However, if they sit in the front seat they are fine. It appears that when the vision to the front is restricted, as in the back seat, the objects seen whizzing by out of the side windows have the effect of causing nausea.

The last cause to be considered also has a parallel in people. Some dogs that are bossy, leader types that get upset when they cannot control many of life's situations. And the car certainly puts them out of any position to control. So, like the bossy child, they get emotionally upset and carsick.

The Corrective Program

The first step, no matter what the cause, is to make sure the pet feels you are a competent leader. To do this, ask him to do something each time before you pet him. This can be as simple as telling the dog to sit, then petting it with lots of praise. This will transmit the message (after a few days) that you expect him to earn his praise and petting. Do not curtail your petting, but just ask for some function to be performed before you pet. It is difficult to teach your dog not to be carsick if you cannot get him to function in other ways for you.

Small Beginnings

Take the dog in the front seat of the car for an extremely short ride twice daily, just down the block and back. While getting into the car and all during the ride you must be jolly, acting as if something good is going to happen. If your pet has a favorite ball, toy, or bone, take that along and use it to sustain a happy frame of mind. Follow this routine a couple of times a day for four days in a row, if possible. Also, do it at different times of day and at night. In this way you are teaching your pet in short, happy rides that the car is a pleasant place to be. If the dog gets sick, ignore him for the time being and do not clean up until you are back home and the dog cannot see you doing it.

When the short rides no longer produce any signs of nausea, lengthen the time and distance of the rides. Do this by five-minute segments. When you reach twenty minutes per ride you then must vary the routes you take. Try a main highway, a hilly or curved road, all the while keeping up the jollity and happy behavior.

Help from Friends

When the longer rides fail to produce nausea, have the dog ride in the back seat of the car. If your pet resists, take along another family member or friend. Warn them against coddling the dog, but have them do the Jolly Routine.

When you have reached this point the program should be carried on for six weeks with at least one car ride every other day to reach permanent success. If there is any backsliding, merely start again with the short rides and you should get things in hand within a few days.

Some dogs have special quirks relative to the direction you take them. If you find this with your dog, do not avoid going in that direction; just proceed at first for shorter distances that way. I recall a Poodle that got ill every time the car traveled in the direction of the groomer! The program of shortened rides in that direction works well in such cases.

If your dog has been on medication for car sickness, discuss with your veterinarian the method by which to wean him off the drug. Sometimes a "cold-turkey" approach works well. However, the doctor knows your dog, and the medical directions must be strictly adhered to for success.

A word about using food rewards to correct car sickness. I have found it to be disruptive. After all, it is the digestive system we need to calm down, and food only tends to excite it.

Follow this program for as long as it takes to solve the problem, which might be six weeks or as short as a few days. Your reward should be a pet that is a joy in the car.

C H A P T E R   1 6

Chasing Cars and Boundary Training

Most of the dogs that become bona fide vehicle chasers have extremely sensitive reflexes to chase anything that moves suddenly or quickly. If your dog has ever "caught" an auto, motorcycle, or truck, you know the serious danger involved for both the animal and the victim. The risk of injury to both parties is frightening and can be expensive. This program is designed to help you overcome the problem of chasing, and running away from the yard, as well as to advise you of the legal dangers involved.

Most communities have leash laws. Check with your authorities. Get a full explanation of the penalties and risks assumed when a dog is allowed to run freely. The consequences have led to financial ruin for some owners. With this in mind, through no fault of your own, your

"He chases cars, and the other day he caught a Datsun and simply ruined it!"

dog may get the urge to chase or run off. This program is no guarantee, but it has helped dogs control the urge, sometimes to the point of ignoring former chase objects.

Establish Leadership

 Most dogs that chase cars do so to fend off "invaders" of their territories. Others just seem to make a game of the activity. In either case, the dog needs to follow the example of a different behavior, provided by a teacher. That leadership must come from you and others who live with the pet. The following program must be adhered to strictly if the problem is to be solved.

Corrective Program

Your dog must learn to earn his praise and petting. To do this, you will need to ask the dog to do something when he wants petting and when you want to pet him. For instance, if the dog approaches you happily, ask for sit and then pet him. This little procedure will start to take effect in a few days or less. You will see the dog looking more to you for directions. When this occurs, you are ready to move to the next step in the program. If this does not occur and you do not start to feel you are in control, it may be advisable to find an obedience instructor who will teach your whole family the techniques of gaining leadership. Be sure to find one who agrees to involve all people living with the dog. Having only one person in the household with the ability to teach and lead the dog will not suffice.

Remove Causes for Chasing

There are several activities that make a chaser worse than need be. These must be removed from the environment before undertaking the program.

Walks: If it has been your habit to walk the dog around the neighborhood, this must be stopped before you start this program.

Urination: If the dog urinates beyond his line of boundary this also must cease. Otherwise, the dog is extending his territory beyond his rightful boundaries and will continue to view cars as invaders.

Fence worrying: If your dog has a fence along which he chases or runs, special steps must be taken to keep him out of that area.

Keep Within Boundaries

The first step to correct a chaser or runner is to establish reasonable boundaries across which your pet should not stray. Wherever this is—the sidewalk, curb, or fence—take the dog (on a leash, for safety's sake) toward that boundary, walking briskly. When within three or four feet of him, shout some word of alarm ("Watch out!") and abruptly turn around and run back toward the house or other area you want the dog to retreat to. Repeat the process until, when you approach the boundary, the dog stops and looks back, or toward you. Be sure to praise the dog each time as you carry out this procedure.

> **Warning:** If cars, bikes, or runners are involved, make sure you have the situation secure; that is, do not run the risk of having a stranger at the wheel of the car or on a bike. Set up with people who are aware of the problem and will cooperate by stopping their vehicle if the dog breaks loose. Put a twenty-foot extension of cord on the leash to allow you to run back toward the safety area ahead of the dog in the initial stages. Never undertake the procedure when risk of injury might be involved.

The Final Test

When the dog no longer shows interest in chasing beyond his boundaries, the next step is to walk with him deliberately beyond the boundaries in the area where chasing has occurred in the past. Make the same type of setup with friends as at the boundary lines, but instead of running back to the home area, simply back away with the same suddenness as before and ask your dog to sit. Keep this up until the dog sits without your command. When this point is reached, continue the exercise about three times per week for six weeks. Do it in different areas until you are sure the dog is responding without your cues to back up and sit. When this happens, your pet has internalized the correction and you can take walks again.

C H A P T E R 1 7

Chewing

If your pet is chewing up things, chances are you have already tried most of the standard remedies such as scolding, spanking, and shaking the dog, but without success. One of the worst things about punishment methods is that they tend to create a breach in your relationship with your pet. The program you are about to put into action avoids physical punishment and will actually strengthen the bond between you and your puppy or older dog.

Puppies usually chew for the same reason human babies chew—to experience the taste and texture of the environment through the oral senses, and to teethe. This is normal developmental behavior for both species. The trouble is, pups have razor-sharp little teeth, which can do more damage than babies' teeth. The pup and older dog deserve the same safety precautions as the baby; put all valuable or dangerous things out of reach. Then give your pet something he will enjoy chewing. Flavored nylon bones, hard rubber balls, and safe squeaky toys are good.

Thousands of case histories have persuaded me to avoid giving things like socks to problem chewers. Dogs cannot differentiate old socks from new socks, or sock materials from sofa material. Young or old, it is best not to tempt them.

To avoid making your pet mouthy, it is a good idea to treat tug-of-war like the plague! It can mouth-orient the animal, so when he misses you he will seek to chew things that remind him of you. Also, tug-of-war places your dog in fierce competition via his jaws and teeth with you, whom he is supposed to respect. I have seen many badly bitten dog owners who indulged in tug-of-war. Avoid it!

Corrective Program

One trouble with chewing problems is that the crime usually occurs when we are not there to correct it. Fortunately, it is what we do when we are at home with our pets that influences how they behave when we are not at home. Most of my clients find that hard to

148

accept, until they follow this program and experience the joy of coming home to an unscathed household.

Before you leave your dog, do not spend the final minutes in a flurry of activity, such as putting things out of reach. Such behavior "wires" the pet for the hours he will spend alone. Instead, sit quietly in the area where you will leave him for at least five minutes, ignoring the dog. Then calmly get up and leave without so much as a word. You thereby set an example for your pet that is serene and unconcerned. If you speak and try to lighten the guilt we all feel about having to leave our dogs alone, you make the animal feel something is wrong. When this highly emotional message is conveyed, tension can start to build. Dogs are great tension relievers; they often chew away all their tensions!

When you come home just reverse the procedure; ignore the dog for five minutes and then greet him, away from the area in which he has chewed up things in the past.

Don't Spoil

Now to the step that is probably the most difficult to practice. If you did not have a problem dog I would not recommend this. But the problem is there and, until solved, you must do this: Avoid all fondling! This is not to say that you must not pet your dog, only that you refrain from the absentminded stroke, stroke, stroke that all dog owners enjoy so much. The reason for this sacrifice is important to understand in chewing as well as in other problems.

If we spend a good deal of time idly petting our dogs, imagine how lonely, abandoned, and frustrated they must feel when we are away. The contrast between our presence and absence is too great. Tension results. And that tension will be relieved, very often, by chewing up things that either smell of, or symbolically represent us. Most of my clients say their dogs are spiteful and get even for being left alone when they chew. I tend, from experience, to think the dogs are missing their people and chew to relieve tensions.

Petting Teaches

What sort of petting is permitted in the program? The best kind. The type that helps to create a better-adjusted, happier, more loyal, and enjoyable pet, no matter what his age. When you feel like petting your dog or when he asks for petting, simply ask him to sit, and then praise and pet him. This method gets your dog to do something to earn his pets. If you and everyone else in the household will follow this advice, all will gain a strong position of leadership with your pet. In turn, this creates a more relaxed and enjoyable dog.

Punishment Is Counterproductive

At about this point many of my clients ask me, "What about letting the dog know that chewing is bad behavior? What if I come home and find something ruined?"

Good questions, but most people who ask have already tried in vain to teach the idea that "chewing is wrong" by scolding (or worse). Also, going through all the antics and emotional upset of punishment only teaches the dog to become uptight when homecoming time approaches. And that can lead to even more problem behavior. Besides, the object is not to teach the avoidance of already chewed-up things, but to avoid chewing intact articles.

Here is what to do when you find things in a mess at homecoming. Ignore it. That's right. Pay no attention to it in the dog's presence. Instead, in as calm a manner as you can, take your errant pet out of the area to a place where he cannot see or hear you fussing about or cleaning up the mess.

If you get emotional and handle the articles in the pet's presence, you actually might be practicing behavior-reinforcement. You probably have seen some children who misbehave to gain attention, even

Don't let him see you cleaning up the mess.

punishment. I have seen the same thing over the years in dogs. So, as unnatural as it seems, ignore the mess and follow these instructions. Grit your teeth, and you will soon see the rewards.

Protecting Your Possessions

So far we have covered the causes for destructive chewing, how to minimize the effects and remove the causes, and how to avoid reinforcing bad behavior. Now let us consider one negative treatment that is useful only if applied along with the total program.

Remember, it is futile to try to teach a dog to avoid things already chewed up. However, it is helpful to teach him to avoid unchewed, intact articles. This is the only negative system I ever advise, and to be effective it must be applied as directed.

About thirty minutes before you are to leave the dog, take some Listerine mouthwash and lightly daub it on things you want your pet to avoid chewing. That's right, most dogs dislike the taste! Do not allow the dog to witness you applying the stuff. Follow this routine for four days and then stop, only repeating it if the dog backslides and chews things that have been treated.

If Listerine doesn't work, lightly spray unscented underarm deodorant on the items and areas not to be chewed. The first day of this routine, and only on that first day, take your pet out of the treated area just before leaving him. Put some Listerine or deodorant on your thumb and lightly daub it across the dog's nostrils, only on the outside surface. This usually produces a distasteful expression. If it does happen, say "Good dog," so as to reinforce the negative reaction. If you do not get any reaction, do not worry. Repeat this process if backsliding occurs. Of course, if you have that rare pet that likes the taste, abandon the procedure at once!

If you follow this total program for six weeks you should achieve a solution to your chewing pup or older dog. Just be patient and remember that most chewing takes time to develop into a problem. Therefore, give some time for a complete correction.

A final comment regarding bones. If you want to leave a raw beef bone for your dog to chew, ask your veterinarian about the practice and follow the advice strictly.

The Logician's Approach to Chewing

C H A P T E R 1 8

Coprophagia

Eating stools, unpleasant as it may seem, is not all that rare and not always abnormal dog behavior. The mother with new puppies eats their waste to keep the litter sanitary. I have seen famished stray dogs eating stools, probably for their slight food value.

Nature of the Problem

Some dogs eat their own stools because their digestive systems lack certain required elements, so they turn to their stools for the nutrients therein. This creates a vicious cycle. In these situations, carefully supervised veterinary guidance is required. The doctor's advice must be followed strictly or else the problem can persist for the pet's lifetime.

Another type of stool eating occurs with puppies. Human children often investigate their feces, and so do pups. Parents communicate their disgust of this practice through words, tone of voice, and facial expressions. With puppies and even adult dogs such communication is limited. The dog can seldom be "taught" to find stools revolting. Once we recognize this, the problem can be dealt with intelligently and effectively.

Dogs who practice coprophagy fall into two types: those who do it at every opportunity, and those who do it only occasionally.

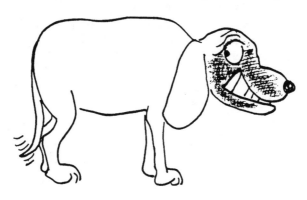

Dogs who eat their stools only now and then need special supervision, both in diet and toilet routine. I have seen hundreds of such cases where the stool eating happens only after the pet is given some extra or different type of food. *Their systems cannot handle the new or excess nutrient, and so pass it underdigested. Since the stool then contains nutrition, it is eaten.*

Corrective Program

Feeding Program

In all types of coprophagia, the diet must be consistent, both in quantity and content. Any changes can produce loose stools and ruin the corrective program.

The quantity of food required by dogs per pound of body weight can vary so widely as to seem unbelievable. I have seen German Shepherd littermates about the same weight, one of which required one-third less of the same food per day than his brother! The clients felt that their light eater must have either physical or psychological problems. Neither was true. In fact, the light eater outlived his littermate by fifteen months.

Feeding Frequency

Another necessity involves the frequency of feeding. You will have to feed your dog twice daily to succeed, probably for the rest of his life. Dogs hold food in their stomachs about seven to nine hours after eating before it is passed into the intestines. Most of them have a natural cycle time (from eating to eliminating) of about nineteen hours. Our domestic pets usually learn to control this elimination time for twenty-four hours due to the human daily living schedule. This is a desirable situation, especially in cases of coprophagy. Since you have to be on hand to feed the dog, you then are also there to supervise his toilet duties as part of your program.

Watch Stools

The standard used for the amount to be fed is this: Feed just enough to produce a formed, firm stool. If the stool is loose or has a rope-like consistency, the amount fed should be reduced 10 percent at two-day intervals until a formed, firm consistency is achieved. Do not fear apparent underfeeding of your coprophagic. If he begins to lose weight, consult your veterinarian. If your dog is overweight, this program may add years to his life and solve the coprophagia as well!

Avoid Punishment

If you have already tried scolding, or punishing, or rushing to pick up the stool before your dog could eat it, you may be in the predicament where the dog will no longer eliminate in your presence. If this is the case, you will have to get the dog out to his toilet area and then remain nearby as unobtrusively as possible. If the pet still will not eliminate, find some spot from which you can monitor the situation but be out of the dog's sight. Be patient until the dog does his duties.

In all coprophagia cases, after the pet finishes eliminating you must **instantly introduce some highly distracting, enjoyable type of activity to take his mind off the stool**. This might be bouncing a ball, tossing a favorite toy, offering a car ride, a walk, even just running happily about the area.

Whichever it may be for your pet, use it with enthusiasm. Then leave the area with your dog, praising him all the way so as to reinforce his forgetfulness regarding his stool. After a few such successful distractions, your dog will leave the stool upon finishing his elimination, with no need for your intervention. When this happens be sure to praise him happily as you both depart the area.

Secret Cleanup

During the program and afterward, **do not clean up the toilet area when the dog might watch you doing so.** Dogs are clever at imitating our actions. I have seen cases of coprophagia wherein this element actually caused the problem; the dog was merely getting rid of the stool, but using a most undesirable method! It is necessary to keep the toilet area cleaned up between uses in this program, but do not let the dog see you.

I am often asked about what type of food to feed the dog that practices coprophagy. The best answer is to feed what the dog thrives on, but make sure the veterinarian agrees with the selection. The doctor knows your pet's metabolic type. Some dogs thrive on relatively high fat diets, others cannot metabolize them. If the doctor prescribes diet supplements, follow the dose requirements exactly, otherwise the program may fail.

Stay with this program for six weeks, and you should experience the pleasure of a dependable pet that will be a delightful member of the family.

Digging

An excellent approach to the problem of the digging dog is the same that a reporter takes when gathering facts for a story. The what, who, where, when have to be documented as a first step. Then the why becomes apparent.

What, is simple: The dog is digging. That also seems to solve the who. But I often find that not only is the dog involved, but other animals and even people are part of the problem.

Why Dogs Dig

If your dog is digging to escape from the yard to chase after or socialize with other animals or people, and if you have tried to secure the yard, you will have to consider ways to change your pet's environment to solve the problem. Ask yourself these questions:

🦴 When does he dig?

🦴 Is it only when left alone out there?

🦴 If so, why do you leave him outside?

🦴 Is it to avoid some other misbehavior inside the house?

Perhaps it would be simpler to get a dog door or to deal with the inside problem. These alternatives deserve consideration, along with the following program.

Our pet dogs are born and raised in the intensely social environment of their litters. They are "groupies." This early life is the basis for the enjoyment we gain from our pets, as well as the problems. Some dogs cope with social isolation quite well; to others it appears to be unbearable. Those that cannot bear it often literally dig for freedom and social contacts. When these dogs are left outdoors where they can see, hear, or smell people and other animals, it is no wonder that they try to get out to meet them. In many of these cases a dog door or simply leaving the dog indoors solves the digging nicely.

Another element can be the owner who enjoys gardening. The dog is a great imitator. If he watches people digging in the garden he often takes up the practice. This can be stopped when people are home, but not when the pet is left alone. Therefore, a digging dog must not be allowed to witness gardening as a part of his correction program.

A further element is an owner who spoils the pet. *Doting on some dogs when home creates a dog that may overmiss people when left alone.* Therefore, isolation will cause tension. Dogs are great tension relievers. They act out their frustrations, sometimes digging furiously. They rarely suffer psychosomatic diseases as people do. If your pet is in the spoiled category, some steps to unspoil him will be necessary. This is probably the most difficult portion of the program to put into effect.

Who's Boss?

Ask yourself what your dog does for you. Will he come when called, sit, stay, and so on? Make a mental list. Then make a list of the things you do for your dog. Do you get his food, water, provide his shelter, open and close doors, groom him? When he wants to be petted, do you comply?

If you find yourself at the beck and call of your dog in everyday life, is it any wonder the dog may perceive you as his servant and itself as master of the relationship? Then, when you ask him to accept being isolated from you or other living things, the "master" will find it difficult or impossible to not get extremely upset and try to do something about it. The picture had best be changed for the good of the dog and owner.

Because our dogs are domesticated they never get the opportunity to mature as wild dogs do. They are forever dependent on us for food, water, access to the outdoors, and the like. It is not surprising that they become bossy. The problem digger must be changed from a bossy leader into a contented follower, at least to the point where he will stop digging.

Corrective Program

Changing a bossy dog into one that accepts your wishes is easier to describe than to put into practice. The formula is simple: Each time your dog asks you to do something for him, you merely turn the tables and ask him to do something for you. Even if the request is

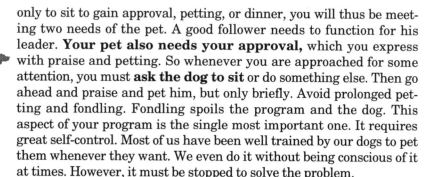

only to sit to gain approval, petting, or dinner, you will thus be meeting two needs of the pet. A good follower needs to function for his leader. **Your pet also needs your approval,** which you express with praise and petting. So whenever you are approached for some attention, you must **ask the dog to sit** or do something else. Then go ahead and praise and pet him, but only briefly. Avoid prolonged petting and fondling. Fondling spoils the program and the dog. This aspect of your program is the single most important one. It requires great self-control. Most of us have been well trained by our dogs to pet them whenever they want. We even do it without being conscious of it at times. However, it must be stopped to solve the problem.

When all of the previous steps are taken you will find a "new" dog in the house within a few days—a dog anxious to please, and more relaxed. Also you will be on your way to gaining a dog that begins to accept being left alone for longer and longer periods without digging.

If you have tied up your dog to keep him from digging, you should untether him. Too many animals have choked to death attempting to escape from tethers. Secure the yard if your pet is digging to escape.

Aids to Correction

A structural device that sometimes helps if the dog is digging out at a certain spot is a piece of plywood or sheet metal driven vertically two feet into the ground. Allow at least four inches of the material above ground so the dog cannot dig into it and injure itself. The only shortcoming to this barrier is that some dogs may switch their digging to a different spot. However, if it is integrated with the entire program, this seldom occurs.

Dogs that dig in gardens or yards often are repelled by substances available commercially. If you have not tried any of these, they often help if used along with this program. Listerine mouthwash is distasteful to dogs, and can be sprayed on objects.

If you have been in the habit of taking the dog out for neighborhood walks, it is a good idea to curtail this during the program. When the problem is solved and six weeks have passed you can try a walk. If it produces backsliding, walks had best be abandoned.

Follow every step of the program that applies to your situation. Be patient and optimistic. Your pet will sense your mood and improve often more quickly than you imagine possible. The result should be a more responsive, better-adjusted dog.

CHAPTER 2 0

Escaping

If your dog is trying to escape from the yard, the house, or even the car, the odds are strong that he has succeeded at least once in his efforts. One success usually stimulates more attempts in the future.

Two basic causes create escape behavior problems: the animal wants to get to somewhere, or he may be trying to get away from something. It would be too simple to say that every escapist is trying to get somewhere, since I have known dogs that were escaping to avoid ultrasonic burglar alarms or just the boredom of prolonged isolation.

One case I recall vividly involved a large German Shepherd that kept breaking out through a window, even though he had a dog door he could have used. After several window replacements and numerous veterinary visits for stitches, I was consulted. I hid behind a fence and was amazed to see a huge tomcat jump into the yard when the owners left the house for work. He stalked toward the Shepherd's dog door, stood poised outside for a few seconds, and then plunged through with a ferocious yowl.

The next instant I heard an unmistakable canine scream of terror. The crash of plate glass announced the Shepherd, airborne and on his way to a back corner of the yard where he huddled in some bushes.

It turned out that overfeeding was the cause of this problem. Quite by accident the tomcat learned that the Shepherd never finished his morning meal.

The cat was engrossed in finishing the feast when I entered the kitchen. I let out a war whoop and chased the offending tom out the dog door. At last report the cat had not been seen in the neighborhood since!

Finding the Cause

The causes for escape may be simple, goal-directed behavior aimed at freedom to roam, to get to a female dog in season or, as in our Shepherd's case, some bizarre circumstance.

To determine the cause you must investigate all the details of your dog's escape behavior. Think back to the first time it occurred.

- What were the elements?

- Where did the pet go?

- How long did he stay wherever he went?

- What did you do when you got him back? (If you punished him back at the house, you did exactly the wrong thing! Even if you punished him on his way out of the area, that probably did not help and may have reinforced the escaping.)

Correction Program

Our program for correcting escape behavior has three phases:

1. Find the cause.
2. Remove the cause as far as is practical.
3. Reshape the environment and the dog's behavior to clear up the problem.

If the cause for escaping is some attractive goal, such as freedom to roam the neighborhood or to visit the corner store for some treats from the children, very little can be done to remove the attraction. However, if the neighbors allow their own pets to run free in the direct approach to these owners is certainly justified and necessary. Escaping the yard, either by digging or jumping, is extremely difficult to clear up if irresponsible pet owners allow their animals to run free.

Whether or not neighbor cooperation is received, some structural changes can be made for diggers and jumpers. For diggers, plywood or sheet metal can be driven vertically into the ground to a depth of about two feet, leaving at least four inches of the piece of material above ground to prevent the dog's digging at it, which might result in injury.

For the jumper, a sturdy ledge can be built near the top of the fence or wall, parallel to the ground and about ten inches wide. This structure makes it impossible for the dog to gain the leverage required to boost itself over the top. If your jumper clears the entire fence or wall in one bound, a small subfence about eighteen inches high can be placed about thirty to forty-eight inches inside the wall. This will break the dog's stride and make jumping impossible.

One of my clients took another simple approach by digging a sunken garden around the wall's inside perimeter. His jumping Irish Setter made one gallant attempt at escaping, but was totally unnerved when his final stride dropped eight inches below the level of his approach run.

Even if these measures are taken, they do not by themselves cure escape behavior. We must reshape the environment even more and pay attention to possible causes before total rehabilitation can be achieved.

Use of Dog Doors

Dog doors are one of the most helpful aids in escape behavior, particularly for the dog that tries to break into or out of the house. They are also useful for a dog that digs or jumps out of the yard, especially if his goal is merely to go to the front porch and await your homecoming. The dog door relieves tension created by the monotony of periods of isolation. **The freedom to go in and out of the house at will** **has cleared up thousands of cases of escape behavior, with no other measures being required.** Some hard-core yard escapists have become content with the freedom to go into the house and lie down in a favorite spot rather than striving for freedom outside.

If your escaping pet cannot be trusted alone in the house, ask yourself why. If he chews up furniture or other valuables, soils inside, or engages in other undesirable behavior, consult the program in this book dealing with that particular indoor problem. Follow those instructions to the letter, and when combined with this program, you should expect success within one to six weeks.

Many rehabilitated escape artists I have known merely needed to be inside their owner's home with reassuring sights, sounds, and scents to solve the dilemma.

Easy In & Out

Getting the Dog Involved

One final step in the program addresses itself to your dog's contentment. *If you do not give the dog some sort of functional activity, he will invent one,* such as escaping the yard or house to patrol his property or neighborhood. Therefore, to fulfill this need you will have to ask your pet at least once a day to do something simple like sit and stay for you. Do not spend more than about three minutes on this. However, this simple functional activity can do more than anything else to relax your dog. You will be demonstrating your leadership. Dogs with leaders are more relaxed and at ease mentally.

Leaders also can play with their dogs as well as demonstrate leadership through the simple sit-stay exercise. Get a ball, a toy bone, or some article you can toss. Throw it, run with it (avoid tug-of-war if the dog has a chewing problem) to get the dog involved chasing the ball or toy. Spend no more than five to fifteen minutes in play and you will be satisfying another basic canine need—the need for exercise and the feeling of joyful abandon that comes only through play. This releases tensions in the animal and increases his contentment as discussed earlier.

Do not take the dog on walks in the neighborhood because that will extend his sense of territoriality. The play times will give him all the exercise he needs.

If you follow the program faithfully you should expect success within days or by six weeks, depending on your pet's personality, your own attention to detail, and the severity of the situation. If you have difficulty, reread the program and investigate whether you might be inadvertently missing some of the elements involved. Thousands of others have succeeded by applying the program diligently. When you have adapted him to your circumstances, you should have a reformed escape dog, and a lifelong companion that is a joy to own.

Fearfulness

A dog or puppy experiencing genuine fear can be pitiful or frightening to behold. Fear causes a dog to respond toward the threat, away from him, or to freeze (play possum). This program is concerned with dogs that are fearful of non-human factors, such as noises, sights, and even certain rooms.

Through the years I have found that the things my clients felt were frightening their dogs were not always the true causes of the problem, but were signals for some other, subsequent event that the dog feared. An example may help illustrate this, and you might find it applies to your dog's problem.

The Fourth of July holiday often brings serious problems. I saw a typical case some years ago involving a delightful female mixed Labrador Retriever and a family: mother, father, and three teenage girls. The dog was a happy-go-lucky type and did not seem to have a

"I'm the lady who called about the tranquilizers."

care in the world. However, when at my suggestion one of the girls, out of the dog's sight, shot off a cap gun, the dog stopped in his tracks and started to tremble violently, his eyes glazed, and began salivating streams of fluid. When this happened the family all gathered around the pet speaking sympathetically, trying to console him out of the "spell." The Labrador did not even seem to know they were there.

I then suggested we all walk around to the rear of my office building, out of the dog's sight. I asked everyone to laugh, as if we were anticipating some pleasant experience. This they did, and we had been out of sight for no more than two minutes before the dog came racing around the corner, wagging his tail as if he were expecting a most happy experience.

The Labrador had just emerged from what is often called a psychomotor seizure, one with no apparent physical cause. To help in this type of case, whether your dog shows reactions as gross as the Labrador's or simply mild fearfulness, we have to recall the first situation in which the problem was evident. In this case, the teenage girls were having a Fourth of July party when one of their guests lit a large firecracker. It exploded close to the Labrador, whereupon the dog tried frantically to get out of the area. When the girls saw this, they got hold of their pet, cuddled him, and tried to calm him, but also shouted at the offending guest. While two of the girls held the dog, the third angrily pushed the boy out the door. The dog was then taken to a bedroom, the party ended, and the animal was literally cuddled in bed all night. Never before had the Labrador been frightened of loud sounds, but from that time he appeared terrified even by car backfires.

The pet reacted rather normally for his type of nervous system to the initial shock of the exploding firecracker. However, the girls provided the genuinely upsetting interpretation of the incident by showing the extreme reactions themselves. They literally showed their dog how to feel and react. In this case the dog responded inwardly by freezing. Other types of dogs may run with wild-eyed excitement, responding outwardly.

Corrective Program

Step one in correcting fear behavior is to analyze your situation. Discuss the first time it occurred, how the pet reacted and, more importantly, how you and others treated the situation. When you uncover all these facts, it will become apparent that your behavior is going to be most vital in correcting your pet's problem by providing a new interpretation for the dog.

If the dog was alone when he acquired his fearfulness you will need to be especially patient with him. This often happens when the owner works and some noise or other event upsets the dog. In this situation, it is frequently just being isolated that produces reinforcement for the fearful behavior. This applies particularly to puppies under the age of six months.

Whether or not you know the details of the first fear-producing incident, the following program should be undertaken for six weeks. Do not omit any of the steps.

Every dog needs to feel he has a leader if he is to react in new ways to formerly frightening events. To achieve this, you will have to prove to your pet that you are this person. As a part of this routine ask the dog to do something whenever he seeks affection and petting. Dogs seem to cherish our approval and petting. If we ask them to do something, even as simple as sit to achieve approval, they soon become highly responsive to our leadership.

Some dogs with hair that hangs over their eyes tend to become shy or even fearful. If you have such a dog, do your pet a favor and tie his hair up, or better yet, cut it off. Life down on the floor is tough enough without having to look at the world through a picket fence. This will avoid visual surprises when people reach to pet or pick up the dog. Contrary to a popular myth, "hairy-eyed" dogs do not go blind when their eyes are exposed to sunlight.

Avoid fondling. When you pet, make it brief and good-natured petting. Long periods of fondling can spoil the dog and ruin any correction program. On the other hand, do not command the dog as if you were a drill instructor. Speak naturally and avoid appearing threatening. In other words, be neither a softie nor a tyrant.

After two to four days of this leadership treatment you will begin to see a pet that is more eager to please, and you can then start the next step in the program.

The Jolly Routine

Make arrangements to produce the noises or situations that elicit the problem behavior from the dog. Also be prepared to produce an object or situation that makes your pet wag his tail and appear happy. Each dog has his favorite toy, or some key word, that causes him to act jolly. If your dog does not have one, you will need to create one. Try bouncing a ball, playing with a toy, laughing, or anything that brings forth a wagging, happy response; even the rattle of car keys often succeeds.

Now produce the situation that causes the fear behavior. But, the instant you do so, clap your hands once and start the happy-type stimulus (Jolly Routine) with gusto! It is marvelously effective when carried out with conviction.

When you use it after a fear-type stimulus is produced, do not wait for the dog to get fearful. Immediately intrude the happy element. Not even one second should pass between fear and happy elements. When you apply the Jolly Routine the results should be as follows.

At first your dog may appear a little confused and even fall into his fear pattern. Even so, just keep up the Jolly Routine for a minute or two, then go on about some other business, paying no attention to the dog. After about five minutes, repeat the whole process. Do no more than four repetitions, twice a day if possible. Allow at least three hours between the two daily sessions. Continue the process for six weeks.

You will know you are succeeding when the dog begins to wag his tail even before the jolly business. If you see any backsliding, merely restart the program.

Isolation Fear

If your dog becomes fearful when left alone, add the following element to your program. Before leaving home get all your preparations for departure completed, then sit down in the area where the fear behavior occurs. Do not pay one bit of attention to your dog. Read a paper, drink a cup of coffee or tea, but ignore the dog. After five minutes, get up and leave, still ignoring your pet, and go to work or run your errands.

When you return home you must enter without any emotional display; say "Hi" to your pet and then ignore him for at least five minutes. If there is evidence of fearful behavior, such as chewing, ignore him and clean up the mess when the dog is away from the scene and unaware of your activities. On your days off you may do this routine two or three times, but schedule at least three hours between each setup.

If you know that certain sounds trigger the fearfulness, produce these on your days off. However, do not produce them and then rush back into the home. Instead wait about five minutes before reentering. By doing this you will demonstrate that there is nothing to be upset about, once again providing a leadership example.

If the dog has had tranquilizers in the past, consult with your veterinarian before starting the program. Follow instructions strictly.

Throughout the program display patience. Remember, in humans, this type of problem can take years to correct, but your dog can respond well in days, weeks, or a couple of months.

One final caution: If your dog might harm himself or valuable property during correction setups, take special precautions to prevent it.

It is tough. . . to be isolated.

C H A P T E R   2 2

Fighting Other Dogs

When dogs fight, the primitive savagery horrifies any mentally healthy dog owner. Some unbalanced people actually promote dog fights, betting on the outcome. These sadists and masochists use their dogs as extensions for their own compulsions to hurt or to be hurt. Even so, normal dog owners can unwittingly promote dog fights.

Causes

"My dog can lick your dog" is an attitude lurking below the surface in many dog owners, especially children. Also when a stray dog is shooed away angrily in the family dog's presence, this can overstimulate the family dog's feelings about territorial protection and promote fighting.

Another cause for fighting is an attack by another dog. Often the victim thereafter reacts with extreme aggression to all other dogs. Two or more dogs in the same household may start fighting as they mature, especially if they are littermates or the same sex.

Serious fighting in family dogs usually has its roots in the way people react to the first early signs of threat displays between the pets. If you will recall these early scuffles, you can probably answer the following questions affirmatively:

- Were the dogs pulled apart?

- Was one or both of the dogs punished or angrily scolded?

These reactions, though quite normal, can actually heighten hostility between the pets. Such human actions do not necessarily get across the right message to the dogs.

When we interfere, the dogs think we are joining the fray! If one dog is punished, the other one may feel we are taking his side. This can make the dog "punish" the other at a later time. Even simple scolding can create this reaction.

169

After years of consulting with the owners of fighting dogs, my records show it was the *owners* who escalated these early threat displays into full-blown battles. On the positive side, however, the same owners corrected the problem by following a program to intervene in a different way with their pets.

It usually takes six weeks to correct the problem. But, if your dogs have punctured each other or have fought five or more times, more time may be required to gain peace and contentment.

Natural Pack Behavior

Before outlining the correction program it will help to consider dogs in their natural social situation—living with a pack of dogs rather than with people. In the wild, every dog has a function—a job. Hunting is a highly organized matter, and survival of the pack requires each animal to perform his function successfully. Injury or death of any member endangers the total pack welfare.

Peace and the pecking order are maintained through displays rather than serious fighting. These displays are rituals in which a dominant dog menaces an underling dog that then responds submissively by either lowering his head, perhaps even snarling as a seeming objection, rolling onto his side or back, urinating, or running away with his tail down. Seldom does any physical injury occur, and the ritual maintains harmony.

Many of these behaviors may also be seen in litters of domestic puppies. They do not persist, however, because the pups are soon placed in human homes.

Corrective Program

You may be wondering at this point if it is going to be necessary to change your home into one resembling a pack of dogs in order to correct warring dogs. No. I have found it far easier and more effective to "humanize" dogs than to "uncivilize" people. However, the success of the program depends on you and others around the dogs. **You must establish a strong leadership position with the dogs and dominate the emotional climate of the environment.** A goodly amount of self-discipline is required, but success can be achieved if the program is followed strictly.

The first step is to have faith in the dog's incredible ability to adapt—to change his feelings and behavior in response to changes in the environment.

In the early stages of the program you may want to keep your fighting dog or dogs separated from the adversary. Also, if your dogs fight when left alone they must be kept separated. When we cannot control the stimulus for fighting, it would be inhumane to leave the dogs to their own fate.

Show Leadership

The first change required is to demonstrate to the pet that his people are good-natured, consistent, competent leaders. Dogs with this type of leadership seldom vie for dominance or fight.

To reach this leadership goal every person in the household must ask the dog(s) to do something to earn praise or petting. This should be something simple, such as sit, or some other thing the dog does well. This must be done each time the dog asks for attention or when people want to give him attention.

Do not order your dog to act; just ask pleasantly, then praise him when he starts to obey and pet him when he completes the act. Make your petting quick, happy, and brief—no longer than three to five seconds.

Avoid absentminded stroking or fondling. It can create jealousies and ruin your program. After about four days of this treatment you should begin to see a more responsive pet, more willing to accept direction. When this happens you are ready to go on to the next step.

The Jolly Routine

Every dog has something that makes him happy. It may be a bouncing ball or some other toy, hearing "Good dog" and happy-acting people, or a suggestion of a car ride. Whatever device turns on the happy switch with your pet, use it as the key part of what I call the Jolly Routine. This routine is used to switch the dogs from hostile to happy moods when they first come together.

The exposure of the dogs to each other can be through glass doors, a fence, on leashes, or in a free situation. You must choose how to do it, based on your ability to control the dogs and the mood of the setup.

The very instant the dogs become aware of each other, the Jolly Routine must be started. Bounce the ball, say "Good dogs," and get the tail-wagging response. Then take them away from each other, or leave them together if they seem peaceful. If they are left together, be diligent and ready to start the jolly business again if you see any sign of impending trouble, such as stiffness of gait, staring, or a tail raised high. If so, get jolly again!

Follow this routine twice daily if possible. Continue it until you see the dogs start to wag their tails before you can apply the Jolly Routine. At that time a valuable goal has been reached—a genuine conditioned switch in mood from hostility to jollity.

Carry on the program for at least six weeks to gain virtually permanent correction. Longer programs are required in more severe cases.

Away from Home

If you feel your home territory is part of the cause for fights, take the dogs to another place for the earlier setup. In any case, be sure to distract them with the Jolly Routine if either starts to urinate. The act of urinating seems a bit like muscle flexing in people—challenging.

If your dog fights other dogs in the neighborhood, do not allow him to urinate outside your own backyard. Otherwise you will be allowing him to extend his territory beyond the boundaries of his own property, which invites fighting.

Always keep in mind the program's principles:

- Gain strong leadership for all family members.

- Ask the dog(s) to earn praise and petting.

- Stop all fondling of the pets.

- Use the Jolly Routine during your formal sessions and if any sign of hostility appears.

Conduct the program in circumstances that you can control, apply good-natured determination, and persevere for at least six weeks. If this is done you should achieve peace and tranquility.

House Training

Believe it or not, teaching a puppy or an old dog to use a special toilet place is a lot easier than you might think—if you use this method. Why? Because it is natural to your dog. Thousands of dog owners have used the program successfully. So can you, if you will follow the directions strictly.

Be a Teacher

Keep two points in mind: First, dogs are able to learn from five weeks through old age. Before they can learn, however, they have to realize that you are going to teach them!

Second, *all dogs raised in normal litters are hygienic.* In early life they seek a spot to eliminate that is remote from where they eat and sleep. We people are the culprits who force them to violate this hygiene. We place doors and other barriers between them and a proper toilet area.

During this program you will use two types of rewards: verbal praise and petting. Tidbits are out. We want the pet to learn for you, not food.

To make you the teacher we will use your pet's need for praise and petting because this is natural. How many times a day does your dog ask to be petted? I'll bet it is more often than you realize. I will also bet that you respond to his requests by petting, which is only natural. Now, however, we will use these "magic moments" to teach the dog that you are a teacher as well as a petter.

Here's how:

• Each time your puppy or dog asks for petting, respond by holding your hand, palm up, about a foot above his nose and saying, "Rover, Sit." (Use your dog's name, of course.) Move your hand back over his ears as you speak. This makes the dog look up, which is the first step of sitting for our canine friends.

• Keep repeating "Good, Sit" until the dog sits.

• Then pet him on the throat and chest with your other hand for a few seconds as you repeat the praise.

174

If not achieved the first time, repeat the process until success is reached. When the dog sits for about five to ten seconds, release him from the command by saying "Free" then pet and praise again. Gradually increase the time during the sit until you have reached one or two minutes before you say "Free." Be sure everyone who lives with the pet follows this procedure during and even after your program. Consistent treatment from the whole family makes a better adjusted, happier pet.

Diet and Feeding

Feed at least twice a day. All dogs do not have the same digestive rates. *You may have to feed a puppy up to five times daily to avoid overloading his system and causing loose, uncontrollable bowel movements. When you find the right schedule the dog will eat and then, within a few minutes, have a bowel movement.* This works out perfectly because someone must be there to feed the dog anyway, so supervision to his toilet spot is not inconvenient.

How much should you feed? Only enough to produce a formed, firm stool that you can pick up with tissue without leaving any residue. If the stool is too loose, cut down by 10 percent steps until a firm stool is achieved. If too dry, increase by 10 percent steps until the proper stools is obtained. If you see mucus or blood, or if the stools do not firm up, consult your veterinarian at once.

Do not switch diets without the veterinarian's advice. Extensive testing has proved that dogs fed varying diets are more nervous, suffer more illness, and die younger. Do not shortchange your pet's opportunity for a full life.

Feed inside the house. Remember, dogs loathe to eliminate where they eat. If your dog is urinating or defecating in a certain indoor area, try feeding him right at that spot (after cleaning it up, of course). Leave the food dish at the spot between meals for four days as a reminder against soiling that area again. Some older dogs that urinate in the house may require this food dish treatment for up to six weeks to break the habit, but it works wonders when applied with the entire program.

When and Where to Go

Immediately after your dog finishes his meal, "scat" him good-naturedly out, ahead of you if possible, to his toilet area. Then stand still and let him sniff around for his preferred spot. The act of sniffing seems vital as a warm-up to elimination. Do not interfere by urging your pet to perform.

When the duty is performed, crouch down and point at the urine or fecal matter and say, "Good dog." Look right at the stuff, not at the dog. If the dog sniffs it, praise and pet him enthusiastically before taking him back inside.

The foregoing routine should be followed after each meal for dogs of all ages, plus on the following occasions for puppies and older dogs that are new to indoor living:

- After waking up, even from a nap

- After extreme excitement

- After drinking water

- After prolonged chewing on a toy, etc.

- If he starts to sniff as if looking for a spot to eliminate.

In about four days the pup or dog should automatically head for his proper place after meals or whenever the urge strikes. If it takes longer, be patient. When this becomes routine, phase one of the program is accomplished: the pet knows where to go.

When and Where Not to Go

During phase two of the program it is vital to keep feeding times as consistent as possible. Do not feed at 7:30 A.M. weekdays and then delay it on weekends for the sake of extra sleep. You will ruin the bio-rhythm of the program; your pet will become anxious and break his routine.

Dogs can control their urination up to thirteen hours, depending on activity, temperature, and other factors. For house training, just as with children, they must learn to "clamp down" to control their eliminations. Once learned, self-control is automatic. To help them, phase two requires that you do not let them out to the toilet area at times when you are not normally home to do so. You will accomplish little by teaching your pet to control himself Monday through Friday, but letting him out all day on Saturday and Sunday!

Whenever you see that the pet wants to "go" during the taboo hours, distract him by tossing a ball, playing with a toy, or any activity that will take his mind off the urge. This technique can succeed in three or four days with puppies. An older dog may take a bit longer. Apply the program consistently and you will win. Clients with dogs over ten years old have succeeded. So can you.

Night Supervision

If it is possible, have your pet sleep in a room with people. This promotes fewer night accidents. Dogs are inclined to become attuned to the sleeping times of their people. If given a little blanket as a bed, most dogs will sleep through the entire night.

If your dog is sneaky about urinating in the house, it may be advisable to take up his water between meals and at night. However, consult with your veterinarian first. If accidents occur only at night, try hanging a small bell on the pet's collar. This will wake you in the night. Then send the dog back to bed.

The dog's second best friend is a doggy door. If it is practical in your situation, get one. It can speed up the program significantly.

Secret Cleanup

Old-fashioned house training methods tell us to grab a pup or dog, stick his nose in or near a mess, and scold or punish him physically.

Poop 'n scoop!

This kind of treatment is not necessary and may even slow down your house training program.

Instead, if an accident is discovered, just whisk your pet out to his proper toilet area. Leave him there while you clean up the mess. Make sure the dog cannot see you cleaning up the urine or fecal matter. *Strangely, many animals find it rewarding to witness their people picking up their stools or urine. They often leave another "present" at the next opportunity, like a little game of "poop 'n scoop." They poop and their people scoop.*

Indoor accidents can be cleaned effectively with a 50/50 solution of tepid water and white vinegar. This neutralizes the residual odor. On carpets, sponge out the area by stomping paper towels underfoot until dry.

Now that you have read this program once, read it again. Keep it handy for reference. Make sure all those living with the pet follow the program closely. If the steps are taken properly, you should expect a fastidious puppy or adult dog in four days to six weeks, depending on your situation.

Jumping on People

The jumping dog, adult or puppy, is a social menace and a very real threat, especially to pregnant women, elderly folks, and small children. If you have tried all of the generally advised corrections, such as kneeing the dog in the chest, pushing him away, scolding, or maybe even stepping on his rear toes, all to no avail, this program should be welcome because it avoids physical punishment. However, to use it successfully you first have to understand why dogs jump.

Understanding the Reasons

Friendly Jumping

Jumping up on people or other animals takes several forms. The one we see most is what I call friendly jumping. *It is usually aimed at getting up to a person's face, because this is the area that communicates verbally with the dog and also emits the essence of life itself, the breath. Dogs and many other mammals put great importance on scenting the breath of those they meet.* They can identify countless different people by their breath, as well as by the body odors which we constantly shed into the air. Many of these airborne chemical communicators are called pheromones. Humans long ago lost the ability to sense them.

Other friendly dogs may have had their jumping problem unwittingly encouraged by humans. Some people love to rough and tumble with their dogs, especially puppies. But some dogs do not seem able to contain this horseplay to formalized sessions, and generalize it to jumping up on all people all the time, especially when they first meet or greet them.

The dog who cannot discriminate between when and when not to jump up needs special treatment and consideration, particularly from the people who have been playing roughly with him. The dog that does not discriminate playtime from other times can become frustrated by the seeming inconsistency of people. This frustration can be expressed by even more jumping.

The answer in this situation is self-evident: The roughhousing must be stopped. When this is done, along with the other steps I will mention later, the problem can be solved.

Serious Jumping

Another kind of jumping can be called serious jumping. In the language of the wild kingdom, dogs jump to place their forepaws on pack members to express or vie for social dominance. Our domestic pups often start this behavior with their human companions.

 This type of jumping can be recognized when the dog jumps and then remains still with his forepaws on the person. The proposed underling is then supposed to remain still as well, thereby signaling submission. Since few respond this way, the dog can become upset and may jump with even more determination.

Most dogs of this type are bossy in other ways as well. To solve the problem effectively, everyone living with the dog will need to follow this program strictly. Follow these directions for sexual mounting as well.

Corrective Program

Our approach to correction is straightforward and simple. **First you must spend more time with your pet,** if possible. Do not throw him out of the house to avoid the jumping.

Most problem jumping takes place when a dog first meets people. To help the pet contain his enthusiasm, you will have to **teach him some substitute behavior that is more rewarding or less frustrating than the jumping.** So, when you and others see the dog approaching, ask him to sit as you move your hand, palm upward, over his head. This will cause him to look up, and looking up is the first part of sitting for dogs.

Tell the pet "Good, Sit" when he first looks upward. Be patient and repeat this process if the sitting is not achieved immediately. When the sit does happen, crouch down and pet the dog on the throat and upper chest. Avoid petting so enthusiastically that you reexcite the dog into getting up from his sit. Your crouching gives the dog a chance to get a whiff of your breath and satisfies that urge.

Involve Others

After a few days and experience with several people the dog will not require the crouch and will substitute the sit for jumping up.

Whenever you and others first greet the dog, avoid overexciting him. Stand with your side toward him rather than facing him. *For some dogs the act of facing them stimulates jumping.* One of the caus- es for this is people facing the dog defensively often raise their hands to their shoulders and say "Down." Even though the voice says down, the hands are saying "C'mon up!" Some dogs actually learn to jump up to the word "down" through this unwitting training.

You cannot control others and their movements, so you will have to teach your dog to sit when this defensive hand-raising occurs. Do this after you have achieved sit to your spoken command. Then, ask for the sit as you raise your hands to your shoulders or chest. Expect a jump or two at first, but be consistent by countering the jump with a sidestep while you repeat the command, "Sit." Repeat this routine until your pet sits for the hand-raising without any need for a command. Then you will be ready to enlist the assistance of some sympathetic friends to follow the same procedure you have used.

After a few people have done it, you will have a pet who sits rather than jumps when he meets people. Also, you will have avoided all of the bad side effects of scolding and punishment.

Jumping on People Who are Sitting

If the dog jumps up when you or others sit down on a chair or sofa, the following technique works wonders when practiced for a few days on a regular basis. **Each time you see the dog approaching with the intention of jumping up, before he is even close enough to you to jump, abruptly stand up and use the hand-over his head technique to teach him to sit.** When the sit is achieved, pet the dog and then start to sit on the chair again. This is a critical moment in the plan because your movement to sit may trigger your dog to get up. If you see this start to happen, straighten up again. The dog should settle, whereupon you must start again to sit.

This little routine can be extremely subtle. Sometimes just the act of starting to bend your knees to sit can cause the dog to start to get up or jump. So watch carefully and react instantly.

If you use body language consistently with dogs you will communicate effectively. And the better your communication, the better the control of your dog will be. Thus, from teaching your dog not to jump up, you will also gain an improved relationship with him.

Try these techniques with dogs other than your own that jump up. As you become more expert with the technique, you will find yourself less troubled by all jumping dogs.

Follow the program with patience and sincere dedication and you should see success within a few days or weeks, depending on how often you put it to work. The rewards in terms of a well-mannered pet will far outweigh the effort invested.

C H A P T E R 2 5

Killing Animals

If your dog has killed other animals, you are faced with one of the most difficult problems. Basically, three types of animal killers are found, and the types are defined according to the dog's emotional state during the attack. They are:

- Angry killers

- Playful killers

- Predatory, cold-blooded killers.

If your dog kills in anger, a complete program can be found for him in the chapter on Fighting Other Dogs, and that program should be instituted immediately and followed faithfully.

Playful versus Predatory Killers

Playful types usually target on birds, gophers, fowl, and other small mammals. This program will deal with that problem.

Predatory, cold-blooded types are the most difficult to rehabilitate and require extreme dedication to succeed. Most predatory types do not eat their prey; it is only their approach to killing that is predatory. Deliberate stalking, lying in wait, attacking the target animal at the base of the neck (a predator kill area) are the hallmarks of these dogs. Their entire procedure can be bone-chilling to witness, since their prey are usually totally unaware of their intentions until too late.

Most animal killers in my case files have a history of too little *activity with their owners. This is often coupled with a history of the owners sicking their pet on stray animals that entered his territory.* Even the innocent act of shooing animals away from the property can be interpreted by some dogs as a license to attack and kill. If this has been your unwitting error, you will now need to reverse your course and appear happy when intruders appear.

Corrective Program

Most animal-killing dogs are leader types. That is, they tend to be bossy in their relationships with their family members. Some are loners. In either case, the dog must learn that you and others in the household are going to teach him. This is more difficult with loners, since they do not show as much need for attention. However, this program has succeeded nicely, even with some highly independent types.

The first step is to gain a strong orientation toward yourself in order to establish your leadership role with the dog. It requires that you ignore your pet completely except to feed him, supervise his toilet activities, and whatever other activities are absolute necessities, such as opening doors. You must cut off all play and petting, and even avoid eye contact until the point is reached where the dog appears frustrated and in dire need for attention or approval. With some independent types, this ignore-the-dog routine may require up to four days before the desired orientation is gained. At this point you can proceed to the second step.

Step two requires that you now show your pet affection, but only after he has responded to some direction from you. This direction can be as simple as asking him to sit or lie down. Then you should pet him briskly with upbeat praise for no longer than about five seconds.

Avoid all soft, prolonged petting or fondling. If your dog does not perform a sit for you, teach him.

Teaching sit requires first that you teach come. This is important in this program. The stay will also be needed when exposing the dog to target animals later. **Teach the Come, Sit, Stay exercise** (see pages 77-79) involving all family members, **for at least a week before proceeding with the following part of the program.**

Introducing "Prey" Animals

When you feel confident that your dog is oriented to you as leader, test him. Obtain the cooperation of the owner of another dog or cat (if they are your pet's prey) or get a chicken, hamster, or other such animal and show your dog how to feel and behave around him. This is where the real essence of your relationship with your dog will become clear. You must be the dog's emotional leader, and you must act happy about the appearance of the other animal. However, before you undertake the introduction, make sure your setup is secure for all concerned.

Here are some ways to make the initial exposures to prey animals. These provide safety in the event the dog overrides your control:

- Have your dog on leash if suitable barriers are not available.

- Have the prey animal on leash or in an enclosure that can not be broken through.

- With small breeds, have a sliding glass door between the animals. This may not suffice with larger dogs, if they charge the glass.

- Hold the target animal yourself.

Whatever your situation dictates, plan the setups so that you can be in control.

The Jolly Routine

When your dog first notices the other animal, you must act happy about it. Get a ball or some other toy that your dog enjoys and bounce or toss it. Dominate the emotion of the occasion. Get your dog involved with you, rather than the other animal. The moment your dog pays attention to you, praise him and pet him briskly. When this is achieved, take away the other animal. Allow three hours to pass before beginning another Jolly Routine.

Follow this plan until the mere appearance of the prey animal turns your pet's attention to you, rather than toward it. At this point you can start bringing the two closer together. You may also benefit from standing alongside the other animal, facing your dog. This side-by-side approach causes your dog to see you with the other animal, showing friendliness. When your dog appears to accept the former prey, you should stop the session happily and remove the target animal or your dog, whichever situation fits your setup.

Be sure not to hold your dog on a tight leash as you approach the other animal. This is a classic method of training attack dogs. Many animal killers will appear happy and delighted to be teased in this way. But, when given the freedom to get to the prey, they attack with heightened ferocity.

Corrective Habits to Form

If you are in the habit of walking your dog in the neighborhood, this must be stopped, as well as allowing any urination off your own property. Most animal killers have extended their rightful home boundaries by wetting their "brands" outside their own area.

If your dog "worries" a fence line by pacing, running, or barking, keep him inside as much as possible and supervise his time in the yard with play. Practice Come, Sit, Stay in the yard to get his mind off the barrier.

This program will require a minimum of three and a maximum of six weeks' practice to succeed. Even then, **periodic refresher sessions are helpful for permanent rehabilitation.**

Leash-Straining

If your dog acts as though a leash is a challenge to his freedom or a signal that the daily sled-pulling session is underway, there are some principles of body language that can correct the problem. The same holds true for balky dogs or puppies who resist moving at all.

Most leash-strainers pull on a taut leash in response to the leash's getting taut. It follows that if you never let the leash pull on the dog, he can't pull back. This is easier said than done, unless you can run faster than your dog. So start this correction routine in a confined area such as the backyard, then graduate to more open areas when you have things under control.

Corrective Program

Take your six-foot leather leash and tie it securely to something solid at a spot about the same distance from the ground as your dog's collar. Then, holding the leash in your left hand at about the four-foot length so it hangs slightly loose, practice quickly jerking and instantly releasing the tension. Repeat this until you do not feel any tug, only an instant's tension. Spend at least five minutes getting this down,

because if you practice the corrective jerk on your dog, his leash-straining problem can get worse.

Now, hook up the dog, keeping two feet of the leash in reserve for slippage. Hold the leash in your left hand, and with your left side toward the dog, start walking in a straight line forward. If your pet starts to go ahead of you, immediately do a left U-turn, cutting him off, and head in the other direction. Let the leash stay loose and slip through your grasp if it starts to get tight. Praise the dog and pat your left thigh to give him a target and to hold his attention, but keep walking. Remember, *you* are leading.

If the dog gets so far ahead that a left turn is impossible, take a right turn (not a U-turn) as you quickly jerk the leash, praise, pat your left thigh and keep moving until the next correction is required. The right turns can be U-turns as soon as your dog keeps up with you more readily. Remember to let the leash slip through your hand if it starts to get tight.

Make the session brief—no more than ten minutes—even if 100 percent success is not achieved. End it on a correct response and praise your dog profusely.

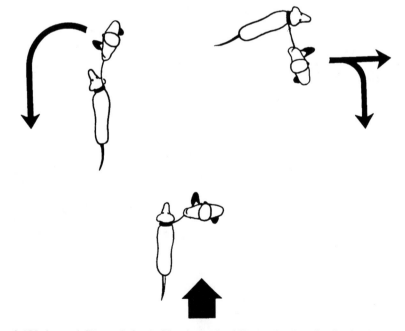

A 180-degree left turn—in front of the dog—should be made when the dog begins to move ahead. If the dog is already ahead of the trainer, a 90- or 180-degree right turn accompanied by a jerk on the leash will be necessary.

Balky Dogs or Puppies

Most balky dogs are either young or have had some bad experiences with leashes. However, the method for building their confidence is the same. It may test your patience, but the results are worth it.

From a position with the dog on your left side, with both of you facing the same direction, suddenly step forward about four paces. Do not hold the leash, but just let the dog drag it. If the dog starts to move with you, praise him, pat your left thigh, and keep moving, taking shorter, quicker steps, which will help hurry the dog. If the dog catches up, stop, crouch with your left side toward him, and praise and pet lavishly.

Getting Him Moving

If the dog balks totally, simply crouch, clap, and praise happily. This should bring him to your side for more praise and another try at starting out. Keep repeating this for three successful approaches, then take the leash at full length and do it again. **Don't let the leash pull.** After a few successes, the dog should start moving with you, and you are on your way for longer walks. In the early stages of this routine, balky dogs may require that you actually run away from them to get them moving.

If your dog starts to grow roots and doesn't move for any of these inducements, try the run-away, crouch, and clap routine. Then stand up and run a half circle with your left side toward him and crouch, clap, and praise from a position directly behind the dog. If the dog starts to turn with you while you're running the half circle, praise him and pat your left thigh. Be sure that during your circling you do not approach the dog or you'll be communicating the wrong idea. If anything, gradually work away from him.

Puppies seem to have a critical field of vision in this balky dog problem. Unless you get far enough away, where they cannot see you clearly, they seem content to sit there. The critical distance can be up to thirty feet with pups less than three months old, and farther in some cases.

If your dog is such a problem that none of this works, it is best to get professional help from someone who believes in nonyanking methods of leash training before tackling the problem in a class situation where distractions can overwhelm the pet. Be sure to secure the services of someone who will teach you to solve the problem, rather than try to do it for you.

Old Age Problems

When does old age begin in a dog? It varies, by breed. Here are the most obvious signs:

- Graying of the coat

- Cataracts

- Loosening of teeth

- Physical stiffness

- Increased sleeping and less activity.

With these as signposts, a student of dogs can quickly recognize that some breeds age more quickly than others, especially the larger breeds, such as Saint Bernards and Great Danes. Little dogs not only live longer, but also show signs of old age later. So, size and health care probably influence longevity more than any other factors. Let's examine some of the problems that can accompany aging in dogs.

Blindness

As with people, many dogs gradually lose their sight as they age. However, the dog has another sense that can take the place of a cane to sense things he might bump into when making his way about the house or yard—his keen sense of smell. In fact, you may have noticed that blind dogs usually keep their noses to the floor or ground as they walk about. This allows them to smell the familiar pathways and avoid objects.

I have found another scent aid that makes life a little easier for blind dogs. This was successful with our Dalmatian that went blind at six years of age, but led a fairly active life for another four and a half years.

Here is the system: apply a scented polish to all upright obstacles in the house and outdoors. This includes chair legs, door jambs, TV sets, and so forth. The dog will quickly identify this scent with things that are "up and down" and avoid them. For horizontal dangers, such as steps, wires, and low walls, apply a different scent. I used to spray such things with a mildly scented hair spray about once a week. It did the trick nicely and saved a lot of nose scrapes.

Voice Contact

As dogs go blind they may appear to become easily startled, especially when touched unexpectedly. I have seen this lead to biting in some cases. So, the rule with blind dogs is always to speak to them before touching them. If this is practiced, you will soon see the dog moving his head to "feel" for the hand that is going to touch him. This is especially true with strangers. When introducing your blind dog to strangers, have them sit in a familiar place and speak to the dog. Have them hold their hand below the level of the dog's chin, palm up, so the dog can find him by scent and nuzzle it.

Some blind dogs seem bothered by having the tops of their heads or backs petted; confine the petting to under the chin, on the throat and chest. This keeps the blind dog's head up and seems to relieve any worries he might have.

Blind dogs may also need "company" when going out to their toilet places. If this is a problem, it is best to put the animal on a twice-a-day feeding schedule and develop a twice-a-day rhythm for bowel movements. Be sure not to overfeed the dog. Feed just the amount that produces a formed, firm stool. Above all, be sure to leash a blind dog in areas that could be dangerous.

Deafness

Hand Signs and Body Language

Whether old or young, deaf dogs can be taught by capitalizing on their vision. *Body language and hand signals can speak like thunder to these animals. However, avoid shouting at partially or totally deaf dogs.* Shouting can confuse them and they often respond by barking. And nothing is worse than a constantly barking deaf dog—everyone is bothered by it but the dog!

The deaf dog must learn to pay visual attention to you at all times when you are out with him. To teach this, get some dried beans and make several small beanbags. Then take the dog to a safe area and, each time the dog takes his eyes off you, toss a beanbag at his legs. When he responds, you must crouch down and make "come-hither" gestures with your hands. Do not lean or move toward the dog, as this tells him to back up away from you. Have at least one of these "pay attention to me" sessions daily, concluding each session when your pet keeps his attention on you for several minutes without using the beanbags.

After a few of these lessons, you should notice your pet keeping his attention on you without your having to toss a single bag. You will then have succeeded.

Proceed to places with stronger distractions until you are sure of the dog's attention at all times, under all conditions. In dangerous areas, such as next to streets, it is a good idea to keep a leash, perhaps even up to thirty feet long, on the dog. This provides maximum safety. Once you have your deaf dog's attention, teaching him to sit-on-sign is relatively simple.

Incontinence

Lack of bladder or bowel control can occur in dogs of any age. Your veterinarian can advise you about special treatments, such as low doses of female hormones for females who cannot control their urine, geriatric vitamin supplements, and special diets. Whether the problem is with urine or stools, the doctor's diet must be carefully followed.

Overfeeding in cases of bowel incontinence is a no-no. The amount fed must produce a stool that is firm. Your pet will have difficulty exercising any control over loose stools. Once the quantity and consistency of the diet are well established, elimination should begin to stabilize and become regular. When this point is reached, proper supervision is all that is needed for success.

Toilet Supervision

Toilet time and place should be as consistent as possible. If necessary, feed your pet in a spot easily accessible (but not too close) to his toilet area. This proximity often creates a habit of evacuating immediately after eating—a most desirable result, since you must be home to feed the pet, and it is little bother then to supervise the toilet activities.

Bladder incontinence can be more difficult to control. If veterinary advice allows it, water can be made available only at mealtimes and before bedtime. However, your veterinarian must approve and set the schedule. It is most helpful if the incontinent pet is taken to his toilet place at the following times:

- After waking (even from a nap)

- After eating or drinking

- Following any play or unusual excitement

- After any extensive chewing activity

- Before bedtime.

Happy, sincere praise must be given when the "duty" is concluded at the proper place. If you focus your initial praise at the very spot that has been soiled, the dog may come over and sniff it. That is good, since it helps to fix the spot in the animal's memory bank, via his keen sense of smell.

In some cases where physical control is literally impossible, the problem will persist. In these situations, inexpensive pet diapers, available from the veterinarian or pet store, can be used to contain the problem. Urine or a formed stool will not be cripplingly unpleasant for the animal.

Irritability

Many dogs grow old with full vigor and remain in excellent spirits. Others, for various reasons, become more retiring and seem to seek solitude or, at least, peace and quiet. Some old dogs object to

being disturbed. Keeping in mind that old age has his own set of behavioral rules, the best advice is to follow the old rule and let sleeping dogs lie. A little crotchetiness in old age is not news to anyone over the age of reason. If there are children in the house with such a pet, they should be taught to leave the animal alone. If this is impossible, such as may be the case with non-family children, the dog should then be separated from the area to avoid any harassment.

It bears repeating, especially in cases of elderly pets, that veterinary care often must be intensified for their well-being, their behavioral acceptability, and our own peace of mind. It is an excellent practice to report to the doctor gross or even mild changes in the behavior or condition of your pet.

As in cases of incontinence, it takes just a little understanding and consideration to afford your pet the luxury of growing old with dignity and grace. In families with children, such a program instills respect for the elderly, one of civilized humankind's most laudable traits.

Overprotectiveness

If your adult dog or pup has shown signs of overprotectiveness, consider yourself fortunate if he has not yet bitten anyone. Many dog owners who see the first signs of protectiveness in their pets later fail to recognize the danger when overprotectiveness emerges. As a matter of fact, some people feel good and even encourage the behavior until a bite occurs.

Causes of the Problem

To correct the problem let us first look at the causes. *Overprotection results from a combination of the dog's built-in capabilities to protect members of his group, whether human or canine, and the actions of the group members themselves.* In other words, the way you and other family members have reacted to your dog's first signs of protectiveness may have contributed to the problem.

In today's society it is quite normal to feel insecure to some degree. Radio, TV, and the newspapers pummel our senses with a great deal of violence. Then, when a stranger approaches our door and our dog shows early signs of protecting us, we may feel somehow reassured. It is uncanny the way dogs seem able to sense our emotional reactions to such situations. And these emotions often reinforce the dog's aggressiveness. In this way we can unwittingly contribute to the problem.

In other cases family members deliberately praise the behavior, even urging the pet to menace outsiders. We see this most often when children are involved.

Owner Insecurity

Another unwitting contributor to the problem is the owner who secretly feels insecure and allows the dog to take the role of leadership. In any relationship a dog has with people or other dogs, one or the other is going to be leader. When the dog is allowed to assume this role he often tends to overdo his territorial and group protectiveness.

As you may have gathered, it takes a bit of soul-searching on the owner's part to find the role he or she may play in an overprotection problem. It also requires carefully controlled emotions and strict adherence to this program to achieve success in molding the overprotective dog into a dependable pet that will properly protect his people.

Bossy Dog

Consider seriously your relationship with your dog: What goes on in daily life with him?

- When you leave home, does the dog try to beat you out the door?

- If you go to another room and close the door, does the dog get upset?

- When you embrace someone, are there any signs of jealousy?

- Does your dog seem to demand a great deal of petting? And do you respond by giving him what he wants?

- Would you be disappointed if your pet showed some other person preference over you?

If your dog is overprotective about you, and if you answered some of these questions "yes," you may be starting to appreciate your part in the problem. Furthermore, the chances are that you are not at fault. It is normal for a dog owner to feel emotionally comforted by the pet's affection. The problem is whether the dog or the owner is directing the occasions and duration of displays of affection.

If the dog gets petted every time he desires, it is natural that he may begin to object if other people come around and interrupt this activity. If he shows his objections with overprotectiveness, and the owner either scolds or tries to reassure him, the problem usually becomes more serious.

In other words, the pet is not really protecting his people, but protecting his selfish relationship with them, that is, his "right" to have his own way with them.

If the pet is punished physically or put away when visitors arrive, he can quickly learn to hate the sight and sound of all future visitors.

So much for the various causes of the problem. The important thing now is to enter into his correction with an enlightened attitude, avoiding things that played a part in the problem's development.

Corrective Program

An overprotective dog requires a program of broad socialization with lots of different people. Furthermore, he needs you, his leader, to show him how to behave in order to build his confidence about people. The pet that does not feel confident about people cannot learn to recognize those with unfriendly intentions. Such a dog may be fine for military guarding work but is dangerous as a family pet. So, take your dog out to meet people, show him how to feel and behave by acting friendly yourself with those whom you know and trust.

When you first meet people, try to stand alongside of them and chat for a while. Do not face them. Face to face, in the dog's view, signals a confrontation. When you are at a person's side the pet perceives you as friendly with that person.

If you take your dog out on a leash, make sure you do not allow him **to strain the leash when you meet people. Holding a dog back from other people by a leash is a technique used in training attack dogs.**

If you have a dog with hair that hangs over his eyes, do your pet a favor and tie it up, or better yet, cut it off. As mentioned elsewhere, life down on the floor is tough enough without having to look at the

"You can bring Fury in now, Mrs Caslick."

world through a picket fence. This will avoid visual surprise when people reach to pet or pick up the dog. Contrary to a popular myth, "hairy eyed" dogs do not go blind when their eyes are exposed to sunlight.

Gain Confidence

If you do not feel confident of your ability to control your dog on a leash, find a humane, competent trainer who will teach you how to handle the leash. Avoid trainers that want to take your dog by the leash and train him for you. Such treatment only makes you seem less competent with the leash by comparison with an expert.

Pet Wisely

Along with your program of socialization, general environmental adjustments are required. In most cases of overprotection, the dogs have pretty well trained their people to pet them whenever the dogs want it. The dogs stimulate and the people respond. The leaders say "Pet me," and their subjects obey!

The worst thing I could advise you to do is to stop petting your dog. But do turn around the stimulus-response pattern of the relationship. When your dog approaches to ask for some affection and petting, you now merely ask him to sit and then go ahead and pet him, making the petting brief and happy. Avoid excessive fondling, which tends to spoil the dog and will ruin your program.

After a few days of this treatment your dog will begin to realize he must function by following your lead, to gain the social gratification he needs. This is good. You may also find the dog more willing to please you in other life situations. He will tend to be less competitive going through doors, more content and relaxed.

In the early stages of this routine the very bossy dog may resist sitting for you and go away. If this happens, just ignore him. Pouting is great self-therapy, and the dog will come around in two to four days. Do not feel rejected. Just wait it out and you will gain your position of leadership.

Use Toys

A final note about your socializing program—if your dog likes to play fetch or chase a ball, use this device with people who come to visit, at the park, and in all the situations where overprotection has been evident. Give the ball to other people and let them toss it to help strengthen the dog's confidence. Act jolly and confident yourself and you will set the best example for your dog.

On the other hand, if *you* do not feel confident, avoid having the session of socialization. You will transmit your feelings to the pet and your work will be counterproductive. Wait until another day when you feel better about it.

Follow this program and at the end of six weeks you should have a dog that is confident, friendly, and still able to protect if and when the need genuinely arises.

Self-Mutilation

The dog that chews or licks itself severely enough to cause injury certainly starts doing it for some reason. At the outset, the reason is often physical, but it can become a psychological-physical problem. For this reason a correction program requires that you follow your veterinarian's advice to the letter. A letdown on the medical treatment may trigger irritation of the area involved and remind the pet to start chewing or licking again. By the same token it is necessary to adhere to the behavioral element or the physical condition can worsen.

Motivation

The motivation for self-mutilation in dogs is quite different from the self-destructive motivation in people. I have never heard of a dog consciously wanting to harm or destroy itself through this behavior. As a matter of fact, the opposite appears more likely. Wolves have been reported to chew off a foot in order to escape a leg-hold trap. The obvious goal is saving rather than destroying their lives.

So the chances are good that your dog is chewing or licking itself, not neurotically, but to relieve some real irritation. At least it probably started out that way.

On the other hand, many dogs start to lick or chew themselves when left alone. Boredom can cause tension, a condition dogs can relieve through licking or chewing. Other dogs just do not accept being left alone. Thence the tension and the problem.

Corrective Program

Whatever may be causing the problem the remedy is the same: Give your pet something to do to relieve the tension. One of the most important facets of self-mutilation cases I find is that the dogs are not required on a consistent basis to earn their petting and praise.

However, after our correction plan is in effect for a few days they begin to relax, become more responsive to their owners' directions, and appear more contented. The way to achieve this is not difficult, but it requires self-control on everyone's part. More about this later on.

Use Play

Play is important in the lives of all dogs, both domestic and wild. People often forget this under the pressures of today's busy routines. So one part of your program is to spend a few minutes a day, in the morning if possible, playing with your dog. Toss a ball or toy, or run about the room or yard and let the pet chase you. Get his tail wagging! This intense, happy interaction is the type of activity that brings your dog out of itself and more in touch with you. Avoid playing tug-of-war, which can make the dog even more orally inclined when you leave him alone.

Defuse Emotion

Another element of your program is to defuse the emotions related to your coming and leaving home. This is not easy to do, but it will teach the dog that being left alone is not all that upsetting. This helps relieve the tensions that can result in self-mutilation. So, before leaving, spend a quiet five minutes or so in the area the dog will occupy when you are gone. Do not pay attention to the dog at all. Avoid even making eye contact. Then get up and leave without so much as a word. This sets a quiet, relaxed example for the dog when you are away.

When you come home, say a friendly "Hi," and then go on about some other business for at least five minutes. When you do greet the dog, do so in an area away from the door by which you arrived. This helps relieve your pet's intense fixation on homecoming. The result is that the contrast in being with you or without you is lessened, making it easier to be alone.

After the self-mutilation has been cleared up for six weeks you may revert to warmer homecomings on arrival, but watch for backsliding. Curtail the welcomes if it happens.

Now for the most difficult part of the plan: To start your dog on his way to earning praise and petting, you must *ask him to do something*. Make it simple. Ask the dog to sit, then say "Good dog" as soon as he starts to sit, petting him when he sits down all the way. Make your petting quick, happy and brief—not more than about five seconds long.

Avoid Fondling

More than any other action, fondling makes dogs introverted, and self-mutilation is a sign of introversion. Do not deny praise or petting, just be sure it is earned.

If the dog starts to pay attention to the mutilated area, instantly distract him with some sound or activity. Make the distraction sudden, like a slap on a table top or a quick movement toward another area. Avoid using your voice, or the correction will become dependent on your presence.

Conditioned Response

After you have applied a few corrections you should notice the dog start to look at the spot, begin to lick or chew himself, but stop before you even have a chance to apply the correction. This is the conditioned response that will tend to be effective in your absence. Together with all other elements of the program, this conditioning is vital to success.

Continue every aspect of the program until the area of mutilation has remained clear for about six weeks. Then you may be sure the problem has been corrected. If you see any backsliding, simply reinstate the entire program for a few days.

If you and all who live with the pet follow the plan with optimism, you should start to notice results in a few days and a total correction in a few weeks.

Shyness—Kennelosis

A shy adult dog or puppy stirs strong emotions in people. These range from pity to embarrassment, but whichever it is, the problem usually troubles owners more than it does the pet. Nevertheless, shyness is a condition that can and should be dealt with immediately, or it may form the basis for other related problems.

Understanding the Problem

To help dogs overcome shyness it is first necessary to understand how and why they become so. *Dogs that are shy from early puppyhood very often live extremely isolated and sheltered lives with little contact with humans.* They may in time become close only to one person and avoid all others. If allowed to mature in this situation they can replace shyness with downright hostility toward outsiders.

Wolves, coyotes, and other wild members of the canine family are shy, but theirs is a self-preserving shyness. If they are born and

raised in human homes and socialized with lots of people, they behave much like regular house pets. The deciding factor with shy dogs, domestic or wild, seems to be the slight amount of early human socialization they get. If your pet is in this category he will need much carefully supervised socialization to overcome the problem.

Learned Shyness

Some dogs learn shyness. That is, they have perhaps been frightened, over handled, or even unwittingly mishandled at some critical time in their lives. These dogs also need a socializing program, but often they require exposure only to the types of things that trigger the shy behavior.

Let us examine the signs of shyness your dog may display:

- Does he avoid all people, including you?

- If so, how does he behave when you approach or corner him?

- Does he snarl, freeze, or wildly try to escape?

Corrective Program

To correct any type of shyness the principles are to build the dog's trust and then his self-confidence. When these elements of your pet's personality develop, both of you will begin to enjoy life a great deal more. The program for overcoming shyness avoids all harshness, demands your patience and understanding, and is highly successful, even with dogs over four years old.

We cannot force dogs to trust us. Trust is earned through consistent and considerate behavior. With your dog, you and others meeting him will need to behave in ways that remove all signs of threat, that invite the dog's approach, that build his trust and thereby allow his self-confidence to take root and grow.

Toward these goals, let us consider—from the dog's point of view—how to remove signs of threat.

Avoid "Fronting"

To animals bigness and face-to-face confrontation are threatening. The human voice may also signal a threat. If you stare, stand

stock-still, smile, or open your eyes extra wide, the dog may perceive any of these as a threat, even as a prelude to attack. Your position within a room or in relation to other people may also threaten a dog.

To avoid the possibility of threatening, a setup needs to be devised involving you and/or others of whom your pet may be shy. In the early stages of this setup, when the dog retreats or otherwise acts shy, here are the behavioral principles to follow:

- Position yourself about three feet away from the wall in the area, but stay within the dog's view.

- Stand sidewise to the dog, crouch, sit, or in extreme cases, lie face down. (I will explain later about lying face down.)

- Try to occupy a position where the dog needs to pass by you to leave the area, but do not block his route.

- Move so as to cause the dog to have to approach you or others to escape the area.

- If the dog trusts some person, use that relationship to bridge trust from that person to one of whom the pet is shy.

- Hold sessions daily to build confidence.

The best way to demonstrate these principles is by example. A couple brought a handsome male Irish Setter to me. They had obtained the dog when he was seven months old from a breeding kennel. The dog took to the wife immediately, but he avoided the husband and all other people. The wife allowed the Setter to get up on the furniture beside her. When her husband or anyone else approached them the dog would get down and run into the closet in the couple's bedroom. Lately he had started growling at anyone approaching his hiding place.

The Irish Setter's condition is called kennelosis, which is common in dogs left in kennels beyond eight weeks of age before joining a human family. To demonstrate some of the principles for correction, I asked the wife to sit on an outdoor couch while her husband and I sat down on chairs beside her. The Setter got up on the couch beside the wife and laid down.

After I explained more of the program, we all got up and walked side by side toward the gate that led to their car. The dog came along, but stayed at the wife's heels. We then turned around, returned to the seating area, and the wife and husband sat on the two chairs while I sat on the couch. The Irish Setter appeared confused by this switch, whined a little, and then tried to climb into the wife's lap. I told her not to be upset or scold the dog, merely to stand when he started to get up.

After about ten attempts to get on the lady's lap the dog jumped onto the couch, putting his head over as close to the wife as possible. After five minutes we repeated the walk to the gate, but the husband and I switched positions. The couple was amazed when their dog again got onto the couch. The husband remarked, "This is the closest I have ever been to this dog!" We got up again and returned, but this time both husband and wife sat on the couch, leaving space for the Setter between them. Both of them beamed with surprised delight when the dog jumped up and actually licked the husband's hand before lying down. Needless to say, the ice had been broken and they were on their way to success.

Keep in mind that during this entire procedure we were *giving no attention to the dog.* No one said his name, made eye contact, or faced him frontally. The pet was allowed the opportunity to make his own adjustments to the situation at his own pace. It took one hour, includ-

A calm and confident owner begets a calm and confident dog.

ing our following discussion about how to make a setup when the couple returned home.

Another example is a dog that was shy, but loved to chase and fetch a ball. The same principles were applied, but the bridge between trusted people and others was the ball. It takes patience, but if the principles are applied, the plan becomes obvious and succeeds.

Extreme Cases

If your dog is **shy of everyone, even you,** it may be necessary to take extreme measures to succeed. When you feed your pet, place the food dish between you and the dog. Then sit down about five feet from the dish with your back to it and the dog. Also, when you are home, take up the dog's water dish. When he is good and thirsty, fill the bowl and use this sit-down technique. If the dog will not approach food or water, try lying face down about six feet from the dish. I have used this approach successfully with dogs that have run away and gone wild, as well as with evidently abused dogs.

These cases illustrate the principles—allowing the dog to develop trust and build self-confidence at his own pace. If you will have patience in developing your program, and avoid trying to accomplish everything in a rush, you should see positive results after your very first setup with your pet. Allow up to six weeks to reach a point where you and your dog begin enjoying life with confidence.

Swallowing Non-Foods

If your dog swallows things that have no nutritional value, he has a condition called pica. Pica is sometimes seen in pregnant women and people with intestinal parasites or a certain iron deficiency. These also cause pica in dogs, and your veterinarian is the only person qualified to diagnose them. If your pet is on a program of medication, follow the doctor's directions to the letter or the behavioral phase of your program will suffer.

Identifying the Cause

Certain factors seem to be common in cases of pica. You may find one or more of these in your pet's background:

- The dog has been extremely oral from puppyhood.

- He will chew on himself when deprived of other articles.

- When the problem began, people would pull things from his mouth.

- The dog enjoys playing tug-of-war.

Although these elements are found in some dogs that do not suffer from pica, they appear with consistency in those that do have problems.

Once pica becomes a habit, major problems can result. If your pet is so affected and has not required surgery to remove something he has swallowed, consider yourself lucky.

Some of the psychological forces at work in the condition need consideration in order to understand the correction methods.

Puppies, just like human offspring, seem to want to put everything new in their mouths. Pups usually decide the article is good to chew or they reject it. Swallowing it is probably the last thing in their plan at this stage. When you pull the article out of the pup's mouth before it a decision can be made, some animals develop a stronger desire for it. Also, *the puppy may learn that taking such things in his mouth brings attention, even if negative,* and so, he carries on the practice.

Feeding only once a day leaves a dog with an empty stomach for up to nineteen hours out of each twenty-four, which invites pica. So it is a requirement of this program to **feed at least twice daily**.

Symbolic Pica

A most common element in pica is the eating of articles that belong to or symbolize the owner. This usually occurs when the dog is left alone, or when the owner merely takes his or her attention off the pet while at home. It is as if the dog were using pica to gain attention, even in the form of punishment.

Note: When a dog swallows something that may be harmful, it is often fed bread or cake to ease the item through his intestines. Another positive reinforcement —food—has thus been given. **The better alternative is to call the veterinarian immediately.**

Corrective Program

From all these causes for pica, you may recognize an element or two common to your situation. Even if not, the following program has solved hundreds of cases and should benefit your dog, if followed strictly.

Most dogs with pica miss their owners too much when left alone or ignored. They strive for all the attention they can get. To make your pet more contented, you will now have to ask that he earn his petting and praise. So, each time your dog begs or you want to give him attention, ask him to sit for you. If he is sitting already, ask him to lie down. In other words, get him to function for you.

It is amazing to see dogs settle down and become more relaxed after a few days of this little routine. Avoid prolonged petting; make it only about five seconds. Fondling dogs tends to make them introverted, and pica is a sign of introversion.

Tone Down Emotions

To help your dog stop missing you too much, it will be necessary to defuse the emotions involved in your coming and going from the house.

Before leaving home, take just five minutes and sit down in the area the dog will occupy in your absence. Ignore the dog, read a paper, or just gather your thoughts about the day's activities. This sets a calm, unconcerned prelude to the departure. Do not even make eye contact with the dog. Then get up and leave without any words or ceremony.

At homecoming, say, "Hi," and then go about doing some other business for five minutes. Then you may ask the dog to sit and give him a nice "Hello." However, do this in an area away from the door by which you entered. This avoids too much emotion in the area of your homecoming.

All of these steps will help eliminate the causes for the tension that result in pica. When we get rid of the causes by getting the pet to function for praise and petting, and relieve the emotional uproar about homecomings and goings, the dog should become noticeably more relaxed within a few days or weeks.

After the Fact

What should you do if you come home and the dog has swallowed something? It is too late to take remedial action. The dog has long since forgotten the act of swallowing the article. However, *if you think something harmful has been swallowed, call your veterinarian without delay.*

When you are home and the dog shows interest in something he may swallow, or even if he mouths or chews, distract him instantly. Clap your hands, or slap a wall with your hand or a newspaper. Do not slap the dog or speak to him, because you want to depersonalize the correction so it will be effective even when you are not at home. Then, toss a ball or some acceptable chewy toy to provide a substitute for the forbidden article.

Never pick up things while the dog is watching you that you do not want your pet to have. You can actually heighten the desire for it. Dogs seem to enjoy "handling" with their mouths the things we handle.

Play Relaxes

The final element of the program is play. This is especially important if your pet is alone a great deal. Toss a ball, run around and let the dog chase you, at least once a day. Do it in the morning if you can. This helps give proper exercise and also provides an intense, happy emotional interaction that relaxes the dog.

Continue the program at least six weeks. You will not be spending any extra time, only changing the way you are spending time with your pet. The largest sacrifice you will make is emotional–giving up those joyous homecoming celebrations and fondling. However, pica is a serious problem, and the ultimate good for you and your pet is well worth the effort. If your dog is on medical treatment during the program, follow your veterinarian's advice strictly.

> Total correction of any behavior problem depends upon the physical well-being of the dog, as well as on his emotional health.

Sympathy Lameness

Nothing is more pitiful than an injured animal, especially a puppy. When it is our own pet, the effect on us can be more upsetting than the injury is to the animal. Sympathy lameness is a condition that occurs long after the animal's injury has healed. A full understanding of the cause brings about the insights needed for a correction.

Causes

Reflexive Paw-Raising

When puppies or older dogs feel concerned about some of life's situations, they often lift one of their forepaws. Some even whine. This behavior stems from early experience with their canine mothers that, after feeding them, nuzzled them over onto their backs and commenced to lick them, first around the muzzle and neck, then down their abdomen and across their genitals and anus. This stimulated their primary reflex to eliminate (urinate and defecate) which is thus a learned reflex in puppies, not a natural reflex as in human and primate infants. During the licking, especially around their muzzles, the still-sightless pups raise their forepaws in an effort to ward off this postfeeding maternal "treatment." The result of all this is that *paw-raising is associated with objection to being dominated.*

When puppies graduate into the human family, you will often see this behavior come with them. If you roll a pup onto his back and gently hold him immobile, you can usually see the paws start rising immediately. If you hold him thus for thirty seconds or so, you can even judge just how submissive or dominant the pup feels; if he calms down quickly and becomes still, he is fairly submissive; if he struggles fiercely the entire time, he feels fairly or extremely dominant. Submissive pups often raise their paws or even roll onto their backs when scolded. Dominant types often put their paws onto the arms of a person who tries to pet them on the throat and chest.

If you get the idea that submissive types are more prone to sympathy lameness than dominant types, you are on the right track. But it does not always hold true, especially if the lameness starts following a painful experience.

Acquired Sympathy Lameness

There are several ways to cause sympathy lameness. One of the less common is to deliberately teach him. Every time the pup or dog raises his paw, give him a reward, such as sympathetic attention to that paw. Soon each time the pet wants some attention, he will raise the paw.

Accidentally causing the condition is more common and usually follows some incident such as stepping on the paw. This brings about the familiar yip, followed by apologies and cuddling by the remorseful pain inflictor. The pain of the accident was real, but the emotional apologetic person is telling the pup that this experience is horrible, and warrants a great deal of attention and sympathy. Depending on the sensitivity of the puppy, the degree of pain, and the intensity of the sympathy offered, sympathy lameness may occur later in several circumstances:

- When the puppy or dog wants attention

- When the owner uses a sympathetic tone of voice

- When the paw or limb is handled with concern.

The latter two reasons are easy to relate to the problem. However, the first reason pops up in rather baffling ways.

An unusual case involved a spayed Doberman that had received extreme sympathy as a puppy when he suffered what appeared to be a mild seizure. Thereafter, whenever visitors arrived and his owner's attentions were directed elsewhere, he became hostile toward the guests. On the other hand, when family members gathered to play games, the Doberman would often fall on his side and have another seizure. This interrupted the games, of course, and led to the attention he had learned to attain through what is called pseudoepilepsy.

Another dog may not have a general seizure, but the telltale paw will rise or limping will start in the affected limb.

Many of my cases have involved sympathy lameness in the following situations:

- A new baby arrives home

- A new pet is introduced into the home

- One of the family goes away for some time

- An argument occurs in the home

- There is a general undertone of stress in the emotional environment, such as, someone is ill or upset and the dog, in his uncanny way, senses it.

Our pets are incredibly sensitive to our emotions, even when we try to hide them. Therefore, since "feelings" are the key to causing sympathy lameness, they are also the tools for correcting the problem.

Corrective Program

There are two ways to correct sympathy lameness. The first is often the easiest: Avoid the things that bring on the problem. This is simple to do if the lameness only occurs when you use a concerned tone of voice, scold or punish your pet. However, when the various triggers for the lameness are not controllable, a different routine must be used. The dog must be taken through the situations that cause lameness, and then you must show it a different interpretation and a new way to behave instead of becoming lame.

The Jolly Routine

Whenever your dog shows signs of becoming lame, you must **start an upbeat, happy activity** for everyone, especially the pet. This might be bouncing a ball, running about and tossing a favorite toy, getting the leash and suggesting a quick walk—the Jolly Routine. **The routine must be started before the actual lameness sets in** and should last three minutes or longer. Then return to whatever activity started the signs of lameness, again switching to the Jolly Routine if there is the slightest sign that the dog is going to act lame again.

At first, you and others in the household may feel a little silly, jumping about joyfully when the dog is asking for sympathy, but switching the pet's mood for concern to one of happy activity will work wonders if you are all sincere and stick to the program.

Repeat the routine until your pet no longer responds with lameness. Undertake this procedure daily if possible, but at least three times weekly until, when you start the activity that formerly produced lameness, you now see the dog get active. When this point is attained, you no longer need to go into your Jolly Routine. However, watch for backsliding. Depending on the age of your pet, it might occur. If it does, restart the routine and cease when the correction is effective.

Take him for a happy-type walk on the leash.

CHAPTER 33

Unruliness

Frustration, embarrassment, and more frustration: These are the emotions dog owners can feel when a pet continually dashes outdoors, or "sexes" visitors by sniffing them in private places. The dog that is just plain overactive, especially when guests arrive, can also be helped toward better behavior with this program. Correction for all these conditions starts with the same step—establishing yourself and other household members as leaders and teachers for the pet.

Corrective Program

Bossy Dogs

If a dog must do something to earn his praise and petting, he soon learns to look to you for guidance in all of life's situations. It is not necessary to break a pet's spirit through punishment or scolding in order to gain control. Rather, consistency and good-natured perseverance are effective and humane. Your understanding and use of the dog's natural language—body movement and stances—also are necessary to leadership.

The following steps are for all household members. Each time your dog asks for attention, ask him to sit. The technique does not require heavy handling. You merely keep your left side toward the dog, lean slightly backward, and bring your right hand through his line of vision to a point above the animal's head. This causes the dog to look upward and back, tracking your hand. Raising his head is the first part of sitting for dogs, so say, "Good sit," when it happens. Keep up this procedure until the dog actually sits. Then praise more and pet him, preferably on the throat and chest. After a few sessions of this over a period of two to four days, the dog should be sitting readily on your spoken sit, or even with the hand movement alone.

Be sure everyone follows this routine with your pet. Use it whenever you want to pet him and when the dog wants your attention.

219

Some bossy dogs may pout when they realize you are turning the tables on them, that is, asking them to earn their praise and taking a position of leadership with them. Such pouting may include going away from you rather than sitting for you. If this happens, simply go on about your business and ignore the dog. Pouting is great self-therapy for bossy dogs. You will notice that the pet's need for attention overcomes the bossiness, and he will return to sit for praise. This may take up to four days with extremely bossy dogs. It is well worth it, though, since the problems to be worked out will require your leadership.

Dashing Outdoors

Many people like to use the sit to stop a dog from dashing through a door. The trouble with this is twofold. If you forget to ask for the sit, the dog dashes, plus the dog never develops self-control about dashing.

The goal of our method, and it is extremely effective, is to instill self-control over door-dashing in your dog. When this is achieved, a genuine correction has been gained. Therefore, movement and body language will speak more clearly than sit, since these are the natural channels of canine communication.

Learning to use movement with your dog requires that you *react quickly* to the pet. This means you must keep an eye on the dog at all times, being ready to reverse your direction the instant the dog starts to move the wrong way. Here is how it works at the door.

Start to move toward the door through which the dog likes to dash. This might be any door in the house, or only the front door. As you start toward the door, if the dog appears about to go toward it, abruptly back away from the door, praising the dog, even crouching down to attract him away from the portal. During the early part of the program, back up at least five feet from the door. Repeat this until you can approach the door while your dog stays away from it. At this point return quickly to your dog and praise him again.

Phase two involves starting to open the door. As you do so, watch the dog! If he starts to break toward you, repeat the abrupt back-away routine. If you got the door open before your pet moves toward you, slam the door before backing away again to praise him. Repeat this until you can open the door with the dog remaining away. Then, once again, close the door and go back and praise the dog.

Phase three requires you to go through the door, keeping your eye on the dog, and close the door behind you. Stay outside for about thirty seconds. Then go inside to the spot away from the door and praise your dog. At this point you may have to start over at phase one because your dog tends to learn by phases before he can learn the entire procedure as a single process. However, if you will keep repeating the process, the dog will learn it within a few minutes.

Practice this routine on all doors and with all household members. Do it in groups of people as well. Do it with packages in your arms and in all of the situations the dog will encounter in life at the door.

Another interesting technique that works well with dogs that dash merely to be with people is to let the animal go out through the door (into an area safe from any harm, of course). Close the door and leave the dog on the other side. Then open the door and let the pet in or out, as the case may be. Do this a few times and the dog soon will look to you before dashing. However, you must then revert to phase one for long-term correction.

Embarrassing Sniffing or Licking

It does not require an elaborate description to communicate the embarrassment of an owner or the chagrin of a victim when a dog nuzzles the private area of a guest. Even other dogs seem to object to such intrusions. The offending pet, obeying basic, primitive drives, may be curious as to the sex of visitors, but must learn better manners for his own and the owner's long-range well-being. If your pet is among the oversniffers, or licks people to excess, this program is simple and effective.

The dog that learns to sit for his introduction to guests is not only well-mannered but also unoffensive. That is to say, people who may be wary of meeting new dogs seem reassured by a sitting dog. Therefore, *teach your pet to sit and to stay sitting until you release him* by saying "Free." Gradually increase the sitting time from ten seconds to two minutes.

When greeting guests, have the pet sit and then allow the new-comers to say "Hello," offering a hand, palm up, for the dog to sniff. In the event your visitors are confident with dogs, have them crouch down so the pet can scent their breath. To many mammals the essence of our being, in terms of identification, seems to be embodied in our breath. Once they have sampled it, they usually are satisfied and further curiosity is quelled.

Following the hand-and breath-sniff routine, have the guests be seated and release the dog. He may proceed to make the rounds, say-ing another "Hello," and then should calm down.

If the foregoing program is put into effect for a few visits, you should notice your pet sitting automatically when greeting newcom-ers. This is a goal achieved by more than half of the dogs put through this program. If your guests will be staying for longer than an evening, it is best to have them ask the dog to sit for them, then pet and release the dog. This places the guests in a position of control and has proven positive in controlling the sniffer-licker. The entire rou-tine seems to satisfy the pet's basic desire to identify by scent, and the tendency to be curious about parts of the anatomy usually fades in two to six weeks.

The foregoing program should be applied in the very same way for dogs who get overexcited and hyperactive when guests arrive. If it is applied persistently and consistently, the result can be a well-man-nered dog that will be welcome in the house with your guests.

Wetting Submissively

When a puppy or mature dog starts wetting for no reason except that he is approaching or being approached by a person or another dog, or even when entering a certain area, the dog is not urinating deliberately. That is, he is not consciously performing the act but is responding on a purely emotional level. Something about the situation stimulates extreme feelings of submission in the dog.

So that we can understand the dog's point of view in what seems like senseless behavior, let us examine where the act of submissive wetting originates.

Behavioral Causes

The earliest submissive behavior that puppies display is seen after their mother first feeds them. She nudges each pup over onto his back or side with her nose, holds him there and licks him from face to tail. The pup's reaction to this is to raise his paw when the mother is licking his chin and neck, which is where submissive paw raising seems to originate. *He then proceeds to urinate and defecate when the mother has licked his genitals and anus, which is where submissive urination has his roots.*

As the pup grows older, gaining his eyesight, the mother merely has to look as if she intends to roll him over for the toilet ritual to achieve urination, if not defecation. This saves the mother time and also prepares the pups to become den-trained when they are able to follow the mother outside for their eliminations later in life.

In its early stages, submissive urination is the puppy's response to a dominant look, but as the pups become more mature they gain some control over this response. Depending on experience, it may never again be displayed in adulthood. However, in cases of extreme stress (from the pup's point of view) submissive urination can recur.

One thing is apparent: your submissive wetting pup or dog is probably not deliberately misbehaving, but is responding to excitement, apprehension, or fear. If you understand this, you can deal with the problem without getting angry or upset. Handling submissive

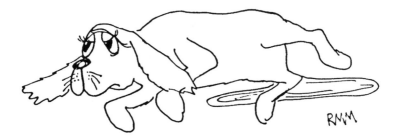

wetting problems demands well-controlled emotions if the behavior is to be corrected.

Analyze the Problem

The problem usually occurs when the pet is faced by someone who approaches, takes a stance, looks or speaks threateningly, or elicits excitement, such as at homecomings. Do a little fact finding about your situation to determine when the wetting takes place:

- When you or others are facing the dog?

- When you lean over him?

- When reaching to pick him up?

- When you scold or raise your voice?

- When you or others get excited?

- At homecoming?

If you identify the things that trigger the dog's urination and are prepared to change your behavior, the problem can be cleared up. The time required will be from a few days to up to six weeks, depending on your skill and the severity of the problem.

Corrective Program

The first step is to **remove any signs of threat** at those key times when the dog wets: homecomings, visitors calling, when you scold the dog, and so forth.

- If your pet wets when you approach, do not approach. Instead crouch down and turn your side toward the dog.

- Do not hold out your hand, especially palm down or over the dog's head.

- Avoid direct eye contact.

- Let the dog approach you. If he seems to be under control, pet him lightly under the chin. If this produces wetting, withhold petting for a few more days and then try it again.

Avoid Talking

Avoid speaking at these times for about four days. Then, see if saying "Good dog" will produce wetting. If not, keep up the routine for four days and on these occasions ask the dog to sit and tell him "Good dog" when he complies. If speaking stimulates the wetting, withhold it for four days and then try it again.

Run through the situations at least three times in a row daily if you can. For instance, if entering at homecoming produces it, follow the program as just described, then go out and come in immediately again, and again.

In most situations four days are required before submissive wetting disappears when you remain crouched. When this happens, you should approach the situation standing, keeping sideways to the dog.

If wetting occurs, go back into the crouch. Let the dog's reaction tell you how to behave. If you see that telltale squat begin, back off a step and start over until you can again proceed.

During the program your dog may gain so much confidence that he jumps up on you or others. Tolerate this for a while, say about a week, then just sidestep, and the jumping will usually cease.

Involve Others

Avoid the mistake of carrying out the entire program yourself. Get others into the act. Make sure you let them know the techniques you are using. Show them. When several other people have gone through it with the dog, it will help make the correction permanent.

When two weeks have passed with none of the wetting, you can feel you have reached your goal. In case of backsliding, simply start at the beginning of the program again. Correction should only take a few sessions.

Throughout your program be patient, understanding, and optimistic. Your mood will be sensed by your pet, and things will proceed more quickly.

Whining

The piercing whine of a puppy or an adult dog signals some kind of discomfort, either physical or emotional. Whichever it may be, the sound is extremely grating on human ears. The cause may be loneliness, hunger, cold, or frustration, as in the case of a dog that does not get his own way.

Understanding the Causes

The puppy that whines when left alone is behaving normally during this first experience. If the whining brings about the appearance of people, even if they punish, the odds are strong that the whining will be repeated. After all, puppies are social creatures, raised within litters, so even if a bit unpleasant, having company is often better than feeling totally marooned. If you must isolate your pet, do not make the error of "rescuing" him by punishment or you risk reinforcing the whining behavior.

Emotion is the most important element in the relationship between people and dogs. Therefore, if you satisfy the social (and emotional) needs of your pet, the chances are good that the frustrations which formerly drove him to misbehavior will be relieved and better behavior will result.

Establish Your Leadership

The pet dog that does not feel the need to get his own way is a happier, better adjusted dog than one who thinks he should be the leader over his people. To fill the role of leader, every dog owner needs to exercise the needed principles daily, from moment to moment. It is a mistake to think that several minutes of training per day fulfills this need. It helps, but unless the training dovetails with a total environmental leadership role played by the dog's owners, more harm than good may actually occur. This is due to the dog's extreme sensitivity to inconsistent treatment.

If the owners spoil the dog as a matter of daily practice, but demand obedience in a fifteen to forty-five-minute training session, it is no wonder the animal balks and is even resentful when faced with such "Jekyll and Hyde" personalities. Therefore, the best principle is consistency.

Is your dog an isolation whiner? Or does he start his vocal calisthenics when he does not get his way? *Either way, the treatment that succeeds requires the pet to learn to earn his praise and petting from all those living with him.* It is useless for one family member to assume the "heavy" role, practicing leadership principles, while everyone else spoils the animal. More confusion results, once again due to inconsistency.

Corrective Program

Teaching to Earn Attention

The principle is easy to recite but requires extreme self-control to practice. Each time the dog asks for attention, or anyone feels like petting him, some function must be performed by the dog. For instance, if the dog approaches and nudges a hand for some petting, the person must, very pleasantly, ask the pet to sit, and then praise and pet him, but only for three to five seconds.

All prolonged petting (fondling) must be stopped for your program to succeed. This practice must be adopted by everyone. Within one to four days you should witness a pet that is more relaxed, actually anxious to please and less likely to get upset when denied something he wants.

Some ultra spoiled dogs withdraw from social contact when the full impact of this program is first appreciated. They actually pout. If this occurs, just let it happen. *Do not press your desires or attentions on the pet.* Pouting is great self-therapy. In a couple of days the dog will be back, asking for his rewards of praise and petting. Then the program may be launched fully.

The earn-your-praise-and-petting principle should be practiced at least six weeks, and preferably for the life of your dog.

Defuse Emotion

If whining occurs only when the pup or dog is isolated, avoid such isolation if possible. If you cannot avoid it, then be sure not to make a fuss over the pet when you put him away or release him from isolation.

For instance, if the dog whines when left in the car, defuse all emotion when you get out of the car. If the dog becomes excited when you return, just ignore him. This is not simple because we all feel flattered that our pets would miss us so. Therefore, we perceive some social obligation to acknowledge the dog's uproarious greetings. Not so. Overemotionalism created the problem, so the correction requires non-emotionalism.

The same procedure should be used wherever the dog does his whining at home, inside or out. Coupled with the overall environmental program, this routine will bring success in from four days to six weeks.

Car Whiners

Some dogs whine intolerably during car rides. Once again, the leader-type animal is the basis for the problem. It cannot control the course of events (drive the car), so it builds tensions due to this frustration, then relieves (or at least tries to relieve) the tension through whining.

If you have this problem, the help offered by the general environmental learn-to-earn portion of the program should be appreciated. Nothing is more exasperating than trying to cope with a car-whiner. However, there is one aid I have found helpful–ear muffs or plugs. These

230 OWNER'S GUIDE TO BETTER BEHAVIOR IN DOGS

allow some peace of mind for the driver and passengers and make it more bearable to ignore the whining, or to seem to ignore him.

The worst thing to do with a car-whiner is to stop the vehicle. Stopping is just what the dog is ordering, next to getting out of the auto, which is his ultimate desire. So just muff up and bear it! When used together with the general program, you should succeed in a few days to weeks.

During every aspect of the program, keep calm, display good natured optimism and you will wind up with a pet that is a pleasure to be around.

> **NOTE:** If your dog whines only when he lies down, gets up, or otherwise moves about or even when still, consult your veterinarian before instituting any correction. If there is some genuine physical discomfort involved, such as hip dysplasia or intestinal parasites, medical attention is the first step.

WHEN YOU NEED MORE HELP

Selecting a Behavior Consultant

Sometimes an animal's behavior problems seem so involved that they defy our ability to see them objectively, which is when the services of a behavior consultant can be invaluable. The following guide will help ensure that you select someone who will work with you in a way that allows you to gain the insight needed to correct the problem. The little extra time required is well worth spending, compared to the risks of choosing someone based on the size of their Yellow Pages ad or the appeal of their titles.

The Selection Process

Have Your Pet Examined

Take your problem pet to your veterinarian for a complete physical examination. Take along a fresh stool sample for a parasite check. My records of more than 2,000 cases show that more than 20 percent of dogs with behavior problems that had not been checked in more than six months also had a health problem. There is no use wasting money on a behavior problem when there may be a contributing health factor.

Get at Least Two Referrals

After the physical examination, ask the doctor about the behavior problem and whether you might benefit from professional consultation. If the answer is yes and consultants are recommended, make notes about each specialist and ask what sort of feedback has been received from other clients so referred. If any of those clients are acquaintances of yours, talk to them before telephoning any specialists on the list.

Many veterinarians themselves are getting involved in consulting about problems, so if your pet's doctor has some ideas, listen to them. If they sound reasonable and appealing, you might be well advised to follow the veterinarian's suggestions before contacting anyone else. But, give the advice time to work and follow the instructions carefully.

Qualifying the Consultants

The telephone call to the specialist is aimed at gathering vital information about how he or she goes about working with owners and their problem pets. But keep in mind, just as you are qualifying them, they are also qualifying you! If they are operating on the highest ethical standards, they will want to know a great deal about you, your pet and his health history, plus the history of the problem from the beginning to the present time. They should be especially interested in what steps you may have already taken to solve the problem yourself or with other assistance. Give them all the facts. This will allow them to decide if they can really help, or if they should refer you to someone more specialized on the problem.

On the other hand, if they show no interest in the history of the problem and simply press you for an appointment, count your blessings, thank them nicely, hang up and contact the next consultant on the list. Anyone in this profession who does not extend the courtesy of qualifying his or her clients through a few minutes on the telephone falls into one or more of the following categories:

- They lack the necessary experience and/or training to do it. Why pay them to educate themselves on your animal?

- They subscribe to the new car dealer's "system house" approach, which states: "You can't get their check and close a deal on the phone." This is not very professional.

- They are too acutely dog-oriented to appreciate your role in the problem, especially if they use the old story that they must "see" your pet before anything can be decided.

- They are too "science" centered to develop a genuine feeling for your problem.

Any of the above types display a lack of understanding about the emotional state of someone sincerely seeking help for a pet. They fail to respond as a well-trained consultant should respond, which is with empathy. Add this to the fact that they do not qualify their clients in order to save time, effort, and money for all concerned.

Get the Facts and Understand Them

If the specialist offers a description of the programs available, listen carefully and make notes. Be sure all of the following questions are answered to your satisfaction. While you are gathering this information, don't hesitate to interrupt to ask for an explanation of any term or procedure you do not understand.

Questions to Ask

- Where and how long will the appointments be? Sixty–ninety minutes is usual for appointments.

- Who must attend? Make sure everyone involved in the problem and correction procedures can attend.

- What will we be doing? Get "operational descriptions," such as sitting and talking, training the dog, and so on.

- How many appointments will be required? Six weekly meet ings usually suffice, even for severe problems.

- Will any special equipment be required? If so, what? This will reveal whether or not shock collars, spike collars, hang ing nooses, hobbles, ultrasonic devices, etc. will be used. If so, get descriptions of how they will be used.

- What is the most severe physical treatment that may be required? This lets you know if ear-biting, kneeing, kicking, hitting, jerking, or shaking are part of the program.

- If the problem persists after the program is completed,what happens? This will prepare you for further meetings and/or charges if things do not go as expected.

- How much will it cost?

With these questions answered, you can qualify the specialist on three accounts:

1. The humaneness of the methods to be employed, which is up to your own personal tastes.

2. The cost of the program in terms of the money, time, and effort you will be investing.

3. What sort of rapport you and the specialist establish. If you and the consultant cannot communicate smoothly during an explanation of the programs, you're apt to have even more difficulty later when it comes to understanding the causes and corrections for your pet's problem.

When you have satisfied yourself that you have reached the "right" specialist, your chances for success are almost as good as they can possibly be. However, after 26 years of consultation work with dog owners, I would be failing you (and my conscience) if I didn't mention a few more precautions.

There are some impressive "silver tongues" in this field. They are exceptionally good at using the telephone interview to gain a pet owner's confidence and a preliminary meeting. To avoid getting involved in something that may not be satisfactory for you or your pet, hark back to the consultant's description of the actual programs and watch out for the following:

- Beware of anyone who says that they can "do it for you." Ask them to meet you at the local lake or river and see if they also walk on water. If they can, check for barely submerged rocks.

- Watch out for anyone who says you will be meeting with their "assistant," and that they (the specialist) will supervise.

- Watch out for people who lead you to believe the program is going to be easy. Solving a pet behavior problem is rarely simple. It requires your mental effort and often some emotional adjustments on the part of all family members.

- Watch out for someone who tries to make you feel guilty about your pet's problem. The problem is the result of interactions between your pet and his people, plus other elements in our environment. Anything you have done that helped create the problem was done without harmful intent. No guilt feelings are warranted, only a resolve to eliminate the problem.

C H A P T E R   3 7

Obedience Training

A Family Affair

Everyone ought to go to an enlightened dog obedience class. Puppy classes can be particularly enriching, but check with your veterinarian regarding possible health restrictions. Please note, I said "everyone" ought to go, meaning the whole family. In this way, your dog will quickly learn to respond to all his people uniformly.

More and more obedience instructors are abandoning the old "one-dog, one-trainer" concept.

Full family participation can help you avoid problems. One family member handles the dog in class, but everyone attends and participates in homework exercises between classes. As a result, everyone gains leash control of the dog, not just the person who takes it to class. Also, if another family member is having special problems at home, the instructor can usually assist him or her effectively during or after class.

Finding the Instructor

Ask your veterinarian to refer an instructor. To avoid possible disappointment after enrolling in a class, telephone and ask the following questions:

- Will anyone other than me or my family actually handle my dog?

- Do you ever recommend hanging or swinging a dog on his leash as a correction?

- Do you recommend or use pain to correct unwanted behavior?

A "yes" answer to any of these indicates that you may experience, or witness, training techniques that cause many people to drop out of obedience classes. Another major reason people quit is a lack of sufficient personal attention to special problems. So it is a good idea to find out if the instructor makes time available for such things. If not, you are probably better off looking elsewhere.

Prepare for Class

You can make obedience class a delightful experience for everyone, including your dog, if you will prepare for class. At least a week before the first meeting **put the dog on the earned praise and petting program. Have everyone in the family tell him to sit before petting and praise.** This is to be done every time the dog seeks attention or affection. Then, make the petting and praise brief. Release him from the sit by saying "Free" after a few seconds. During the week, two or three times a day, stand with the dog at your left

side, tell him to sit, and gradually extend the time of the sit until he will stay still for two minutes.

This simple exercise will give you a valuable head start on life in obedience class, where you will be expected to hold your dog's attention in spite of distractions of other dogs and people.

Helpful Reading

Campbell, W. E.: *Behavior Problems in Dogs.* Moseby Yearbook Publi cations, Santa Barbara, 1975.

Mery, F.: *The Life, History and Magic of the Dog.* Grossett & Dunlop, New York, 1970.

Scott, J.P. and Fuller, J.P.: *Dog Behavior: The Genetic Basis.* University of Chicago Press, 1965.

Shah, I.: *The Sufis.* Doubleday, New York, 1962.

Tuttle, J. L., editor: *Dogs Need Our Love.* Libra, Roslyn Heights, NY, 1983.

Index

Your Comments are Invited

If you enjoyed *Owner's Guide to Better Behavior In Dogs* or found it especially helpful, we would like to hear from you. If you want to comment on any aspect of the book, feel free to do so. Just write:

Editorial Office
Alpine Publications
225 S. Madison Ave.
Loveland, CO 80537

For a Free Catalog of Alpine Books

or for information on other Alpine Blue Ribbon titles, please write to our Customer Service Department, P. O. Box 7027, Loveland, CO 80537, or call toll free 1-800-777-7257.

Additional Titles of Interest:

How to Raise a Puppy You Can Live With
Clarice Rutherford and David H. Neil, MRCVS
This book is a "must" for every breeder, as well as for new puppy owners! Behavior shaping and socialization for dog's first year.

The Mentally Sound Dog
Gail Clark, Ph.D. and William Boyer, Ph.D.
More on canine behavior, training, and development.

Positively Obedient: Good Manners for the Family Dog
Barbara Handler
Basic training and manners, written by an obedience instructor.

201 Ways to Enjoy Your Dog: Guide to Organized Activities
Ellie Milon
The answer to many behavior problems is giving your dog something to do. Learn how and where to get started.